MAKE
YOUR OWN
BREAKS

To Harold, Vicky + family

– At long last –
the book! The only thing
that takes longer than
producing a book is clearing
paperwork with Transport Canada!
Hope you like it –
Thanks again + hope
you have a great
year!

P.S.
[signature]
Don p s

MAKE YOUR OWN BREAKS

BECOME AN ENTREPRENEUR & CREATE YOUR OWN FUTURE

JIM LANG

Trifolium Books Inc.
TORONTO

Make Your Own Breaks
Become an Entrepreneur and Create Your Own Future

First published in 1994 by
Trifolium Books Inc.
238 Davenport Road
Suite 28
Toronto, Ontario
M5R 1J6
Canada

Canadian Cataloguing in Publication Data

Lang, Jim, 1947-
Make your own breaks : become an entrepreneur and create your own future

Includes biographical references.
ISBN 1-895579-28-7

1. Entrepreneurship. 2. Entrepreneurship - Problems, exercises, etc. 3. Entrepreneurship - Canada - Case studies. I. Title.

HB615.L36 1994   658.4'21   C94-930165-5

Ordering Information
Orders by Canadian trade bookstores, wholesalers, individuals, organizations, and for quantity sales. Please contact Stoddart Publishing Co. Limited, 34 Lesmill Road, Don Mills, Ontario, Canada M3B 2T6; tel. Ontario and Quebec (800) 387-0141, all other provinces (800) 387-0172; fax (416) 445-5967.

Orders for course adoption/educational use: Please contact Trifolium Books Inc., 238 Davenport Road, Suite 28, Toronto, Ontario, Canada M5R 1J6; tel. (416) 925-0765; fax (416) 925-2360.

Design/Illustrations: Jack Steiner Graphic Design
Editing: Susan Lawrence
Production: Francine Geraci
Credit: Canadian Foundation for Economic Education: p. 163, Decision-making grid.

Printed in Canada at Webcom
Printed on acid-free paper.
Last digit is print number: 10 9 8 7 6 5 4 3 2 1

Cover photo of Jim Lang by Mike Price

Contents

Foreword

I spend a lot of time on speaking engagements telling thousands of people about entrepreneurship and I've always wished I had a book that would explain what I'm trying to say. Finally there is one: *Make Your Own Breaks* is that book.

Make Your Own Breaks defines entrepreneurship in a way everyone can relate to. It's a commonsense, straightforward basic approach that takes the mystery out of starting your own business venture. There's no magic involved; you just have to work! *Make Your Own Breaks* answers all the tough questions. Anyone in business, or wanting to be in business, needs to read this book.

I've worked hard to become a successful entrepreneur and I enjoy the benefits that success has given me. But what I enjoy even more is seeing other people eagerly trying to become entrepreneurs. I know they can do it because I did it, and I wasn't particularly good in school.

I didn't have anyone to teach me how to become an entrepreneur; I had to learn by doing. And once I got going, I didn't have much time to sit around and wonder just how I became who I am. Fortunately, entrepreneurship is now being taught — to high school and college students and to adults. If they'd had courses like these when I was in school, I think I'd have been a lot more attentive.

I love being an entrepreneur and I want more people to enjoy life the way I do. But there's an even more important reason to encourage people in this area. The world is changing rapidly, from one where you could get a secure job for life, to one where it seems no job is secure. In the future, people seeking security will have to find it inside themselves. Instead of demanding jobs from other people, entrepreneurs take their economic fate into their own hands. They take control of their own lives. That's what becoming an entrepreneur is really all about. And that's what the future is all about.

Make Your Own Breaks is really a guide to surviving and thriving in the restructured world of the 1990s and beyond, to the next millennium. I believe we're about to enter the golden age of entrepreneurship and this book is pointing the way.

Ron Foxcroft
President
Fortron International Inc.

Acknowledgments

Entrepreneurs rarely accomplish anything without the help of others, and I am humbled by being no different from most in that respect. My wife, Mary Ackroyd, stands out among those who have encouraged and assisted me in this book. She reviewed every word, her advice unerring and her perspective unique. Together we have lurched, stumbled, and soared through various enterprises. As we learned new lessons of entrepreneurship, Mary would say, "You really must write this down, some day."

For creating the primary concepts upon which this book is based, and for their insights and pioneering contributions to teaching entrepreneurship, I thank Larry Smith, Tom Tidey, Lori Cranson, William Jennings, and the late, wonderful Lily Kretchman. Special to that group is Gary Rabbior, who has provided me with many opportunities to practice what I preach. Thanks also to teachers John Ekins and George Pineau for their assistance in reviewing the exercises.

I am also indebted to the 42 entrepreneurs who participated in this book. They offered freely not only their time and experience, but their enthusiastic support of the book. I thank Michael Vaughan and Tier One Communications for the opportunity to meet most of these entrepreneurs in the first place.

Who better to publish a book on entrepreneurship than Trifolium Books Inc., a trio of entrepreneurs? I thank my partners in this venture: Trudy Rising, Mary Kay Winter, and especially, Grace Deutsch, to whom I first confessed my desire to write such a book. To my amazement, she encouraged me. I thank her for that, and for her unwaivering belief in the importance of our work. Not least, I wish to thank Susan Lawrence for excising editorial warts and turning the manuscript into the book you hold in your hands. Of course, any errors or oversights are mine alone.

Finally, I would like to thank my son, John, for generously sharing his dad — and the computer — with this project.

Dedication

To entrepreneurs and would-be entrepreneurs everywhere. Through your efforts and initiative, the future is yours.

I also want to dedicate this book to the memory of Lily Kretchman — educator, visionary, and friend. Her belief in the power of entrepreneurship education imbued all who knew her with a profound desire to continue her legacy.

Introduction

Thank you for selecting this book. You're holding a piece of my life in your hands. You see, I'm an entrepreneur and this book is one of my ventures. Even though I can't see you, I can imagine you reading these lines and I am thrilled at the thought. I am experiencing success through your act of choosing buying this book.

"Of course, you are," you say. "You got my money!" You're partly right. My publishers—who are entrepreneurs just like me—spent a bundle getting this book into your hands, and I spent months hammering at the text until we all agreed it said what I wanted it to say, so, yes, now we're pleased we're all going to get paid. But, if I just wanted to make money, there are other ways for me to make a great deal more than I'm likely to make from selling you this book. I don't just want your money. I want YOU!

Now, don't panic. I'm not a fanatic or cult leader. But I do want to win you over to an exciting and fulfilling way of life. I want you to become an entrepreneur, so that you can experience the freedom, satisfaction, and day-to-day excitement that I—and all the entrepreneurs you'll meet in this book—enjoy.

Maybe you're thinking, "Hey, if I had your money, I'd probably be as happy as you are." In monetary terms, I am comfortably off, but not what I'd call rich. But, I *am* as successful as anyone you care to name. I am extremely happy and I enjoy life. And it's because I've learned how to be an entrepreneur. At this point I wouldn't blame you if you thought, "Nice for you. You were probably lucky enough to be born that way." Well, you're wrong. I was *not* born an entrepreneur. I don't think anyone ever is born an entrepreneur. I *became* an entrepreneur and, if I could do it, so can you!

You already have what it takes. Like all of us, you were born a risk-taker. You risked skinned knees because you wanted to walk, not crawl, and to ride your bike, not walk. I'm asking you to rediscover that childlike courage and to take a risk.

I'm asking you to risk your life on your dreams and abilities. I know you have some dreams and abilities—everybody does, and, if you'll work through this book with me, I'll prove that to you. You don't have to risk whatever security you now have. You can take your time and grow into your new life at your own pace—and you'll learn how to manage risk so that you won't lose anything of real value. You *will* lose any fear of change or insecurity you may now have and you will lose any feelings of not being in control of your life. Good riddance! And look at what you'll gain — control of your life. You'll learn to embrace change and weave it into the fabric of your daily life. You'll learn to love life and, as a bonus, you'll make money—perhaps a *lot* of it. I can't say it will be easy for you to become an entrepreneur. It wasn't easy for me. But, I am saying, emphatically, that no matter who you are; no matter what you're now doing or once did; no matter who your parents are or what they do or did; no matter how old or young you are or what color you may be; no matter if you are female, male, physically disabled or not—you can learn to become an entrepreneur *and it is worth it!*

This book is unique. Why? It's for everyone who is not yet an entrepreneur. There are plenty of guidebooks available for full-blown entrepreneurs. These books offer you surefire opportunities for the 1990s; they tell you how to be a better manager; how to avoid common business pitfalls; how to find and use financial advice; and how to identify lucrative markets. Each book offers a piece of the puzzle, and many do a very good job. But all these books are aimed at people who already consider themselves entrepreneurs and who are already involved in one or more ventures. And these books often reflect the common misconception that entrepreneurs are born, not made.

This is *not* true. Entrepreneurs are people like you, who have learned to do what they do. This is quite a new concept.

In recent years, researchers, academics, and educators have discovered that entrepreneurship is really a systematic process that can be learned and taught. In the past, most business research was focused on studying enterprises or businesses. The new research undertook to study entrepreneurs— how they go about living their lives and how they initiate and run their ventures. Researchers found that entrepreneurs share common characteristics, such as self-confidence, persistence, and the need to achieve. Entrepreneurs also share certain skills, such as communication, team building, and planning, and they tend to use these skills in similar ways. It became clear that anyone could learn to become an entrepreneur, and furthermore, that the process of entrepreneurship is not limited to the world of business, but could be applied to any human endeavor.

When educators got hold of this research, they said, "If entrepreneurship can be learned, it can be taught. We can teach all of this!" Today, thousands of high school and college students are learning to become entrepreneurs by taking accredited courses in entrepreneurship. Self-confident and armed with new skills and knowledge, a whole new generation of entrepreneurs is being created.

I'm an entrepreneur, but I had to learn the hard way, over a period of 20 years. I made the same mistakes most other entrepreneurs make. *You* don't have to do what I did. You don't have to repeat the mistakes of others. By using this new knowledge, you will be free to soar with your imagination; you won't have to fly by the seat of your pants. Life is not a straight line from birth to death, and mine is no exception. But after I became an entrepreneur, I chose each turn, each new direction, and I became addicted to being in control of my life. Part of me is a teacher, so I use my teaching skills to help others learn to take control of their lives the way I control mine. When I was exposed to the new entrepreneurship curriculum, my entrepreneurial life became truly focused for the first time. Here was a description of me! Here was a clear, systematic, and effective way to teach others what I had been trying to teach for years. Here was something truly powerful.

Make Your Own Breaks is the first book that teaches you how to become an entrepreneur. If you already consider yourself an entrepreneur, this book can help you avoid the usual pitfalls and speed your progress to your goals. I know I can teach and I know you can learn.

Here are some more ways in which this book is unique. This book will not teach you how to get rich quickly—there's no surefire route for that. But, it *will* help you lead a rich life. This book will not show you how to do a detailed venture plan or a detailed strategic plan for the venture (although you'll find a sample venture plan in the appendix). There are lots of other books that can do that for you. It *will* show you why planning is important, so you'll be motivated to plan, when the time comes. This book is not merely about how to get started in a small business—lots of books do that. This book is about opening the door to entrepreneurship for *you*, and not just to small business—to any venture you can dream of.

Make Your Own Breaks is not only the title of this book. It's also what you have to do. You have to do the work. But you won't be alone. I have enlisted 42 entrepreneurs to help guide you on your journey. Many of them are new friends of mine, and all of them are kindred spirits. Welcome to our world.

How to Use This Book

Meet your new teacher—YOU!

Today thousands of high school and college students are learning how to become entrepreneurs before they jump into their first venture. This new approach to entrepreneurship education is now available to you—through this book. Just start at the beginning and work your way through.

Take your time—and work hard

Be patient and deliberate with yourself. If necessary, repeat the most challenging activities until you are comfortable with them. Apply self-discipline and be prepared to work. Reading alone will not turn you into an entrepreneur. Entrepreneurs are doers. You have to do the exercises and activities in order to develop necessary skills.

Use the whole book, not just the juicy parts

If you like to skim through a book, resist that urge. The sequence of the book is significant. Certain attitudes and skills must be understood and developed before the next steps are taken. Very often the problems entrepreneurs encounter result from pushing the process. Be a good teacher and stick to the lesson plans.

Understand the format and terms

This book is structured to help you stay focused on what you are trying to achieve and why, how you will achieve it, and how you will know when you have succeeded. As you work through each chapter, you will find information that will help you understand the reasons for the assigned tasks. This information is organized in two ways:

Profiles: True stories about actual entrepreneurs
Key Points: One-line important reminders

You'll also find exercises, each with a stated objective and task, and an evaluation guide to help you measure your progress. At the back of the book are a sample venture plan and a list of helpful books, magazines, and associations. You'll find everything you need to learn to get started as a new entrepreneur.

Get to Know Yourself

"The unexamined life is not worth living."

    & SOCRATES

The word "entrepreneur" means different things to different people. You probably had an image in your mind when you picked up this book. Perhaps you see entrepreneurs as confident, positive, successful, energetic, and fulfilled people. The entrepreneur's ability to put an upbeat spin on problems or challenges may match your own approach to life, or it may be a picture of what you want to become. Whatever your perspective, most people would agree that entrepreneurs seem to be in charge of their own lives and that's an attractive quality.

To become an entrepreneur you first need to know what entrepreneurs are like. In this chapter, you'll learn:

• what motivates entrepreneurs

• what personal characteristics entrepreneurs share

• how entrepreneurs manage risk

• what you're like and what you like to do

• how to assess and measure your entrepreneurial abilities.

What are entrepreneurs like? What makes them tick? To get an idea, meet Harold Warner.

PRO FILE

Entrepreneur: Harold Warner

Enterprise: AeroDynamics Aerostats and Promotions Inc.

Harold Warner thought he was a real estate salesperson. After all, he was selling real estate and doing quite well at it. The economy was booming;

Harold and his wife were expecting their first child and his Dream Development Deal was about to become reality. The money would roll in and he would take his happy

▶ ▶ ▶ ▶▶▶▶▶

family out with him to pursue his private passion—hot air ballooning. Life would be good. Then the phone rang...

"The guy at the other end of the line was trying to tell me the deal was dead," Harold recalls. "I knew the deal was a sure thing. I had invested everything in it and this had to be a bad joke. But it wasn't a joke. Suddenly I was broke—worse than broke, I was in debt, too." As if on cue, the boom went bust and the real estate market deflated like a popped balloon.

Harold had little to fall back on. He had not been a good student in his youth. He lived for the active life, especially sports. He had entertained himself and his classmates by playing the class clown. "How could you be expected to pay attention to the teacher when you could hear the cheers from the football field?" Harold couldn't. He had dropped out of high school.

There were no new jobs waiting for Harold Warner in his time of crisis. "I had to take a good look at myself. What am I? What possible skill do I have that I could sell? I had to get down to the most fundamental level, to a level where no banker could foreclose. I decided that I

might as well do the one thing I had reserved for fun—fly the balloon."

With no other options apparent, it made sense to do the one thing he enjoyed the most. He began to sell advertising space on his balloon. Soon he had a small income and could hire another pilot and another balloon. It didn't seem like work because it was his greatest passion. Today Harold's company, AeroDynamics Aerostats and Promotions Inc., flies balloons all over the world and employs as many as 76 people, including pilots, support staff, and maintenance engineers. Harold makes a good living, his debts are under control, and he lives well.

"In spite of how horrible it was at the time, I still consider that moment of complete defeat, and the realization that I had to completely rebuild my life, the greatest moment of my life. You know, I look at Wayne Gretzky and Jack Nicklaus and I say they are no more successful than I am. They are wealthier than I am, but they are no more successful. I am successful because I am doing what I was meant to do. And that is what success is, doing what you were meant to do."

Harold Warner discovered who he really was when he was at the lowest point in his life. Through entrepreneurship he took creative control over his own life; he set his own goals and discovered his own definition of success.

 KEY POINT   **Entrepreneurs know who they are**

How Do You Define Yourself?

Does your job define you? Do you say, "I am a bank teller" and mean that's what you *really* are? Or are you simply defining your current occupation?

There is a difference. Do you like your job but want more responsibility? Are you excited by your work environment but would like more ownership? Would you like to change your work and your life completely? It may be time to take a systematic look at your expectations of life in general and of your working life in particular.

Get to know yourself

Who are you, really? It sounds simple. Surely we all know who we are, don't we? Not necessarily. We seem ready to accept that it takes a lot of work and time to get to know our children or our mate. We are prepared to spend hours, days, and months learning new skills and getting to know a new job. How odd that we assume self-knowledge is automatic when no other kind of knowledge comes without effort.

You can become self-aware by studying yourself the way you study others—by observation. For example, how do you react to challenges and changes? Do you like to try new ways of doing things or do you prefer to keep to a set routine? Are you frustrated by things that don't work, poor service, or the lack of certain products, or do you just accept the status quo? Try not to be judgmental. Just observe, for now.

The kind of self-awareness advocated here is not directed at curing dysfunctions or exorcising childhood demons—there are other, more pertinent self-help groups operating in those arenas. You are who you are. There is no attempt here to impose values or assess relationships or heal any dysfunctions. Entrepreneurship will require particularly hard work and some fundamental realignment of values for anyone with a "victim" mentality. But the essence of entrepreneurship is that each entrepreneur is unique and each enterprise is tailored exclusively to that individual.

How did you become who you are?

When you look in the mirror you see someone who has been shaped by many factors: heredity, environment, tragedy, joy, failure, and success. You can't change your genes and you had little control over your childhood, but most of the person you see in the mirror is someone you created.

Every waking moment is filled with options. Some are simple, almost trivial: Eat this or that? Wear this or that? Walk or drive? Others are more important: Stay in school or get a job? Get married to this person, that person, or stay single? Have a child or two or none? Keep this job or get another? Give up or persevere? As you examine the choices you've made, you may agree that you have had more control over your life than you thought. As you become more entrepreneurial, you will recognize your ability to shape your life through your decisions.

Who's in charge here?

As an entrepreneur you will see your life as the sum total of your choices and decisions. You will revel, guilt free, in your successes, and you will recognize, soberly and fully, your failures. You will rarely waste time finding and laying blame except as it pertains to future decisions. If you don't take time to reflect on your life regularly, you may well be carrying a bundle of false, or at least, poorly based, assumptions about yourself; assumptions that could lead to some poor choices at best, and a long and hard route to your goals at worst.

You'll learn more about developing decision-making skills later on, but for now it's enough to recognize that you are now living through the consequences of your earlier decisions. You may be embarrassed to think about how little thought went into decisions that had ultimately had a big effect on your life. If so, you aren't alone. It is frightening to hear college students explain their career choices. For example, one said, "I saw a law show on TV one day and, like, lawyers make mega bucks and, like, I like money, so I went into law." Thousands of dollars and seven years later, a confused and disappointed young lawyer may realize that law is nothing like what he expected.

 Entrepreneurs see themselves as the product of their choices

It's time to take a look at where your choices have taken you and see how they match your image of yourself.

EXERCISE 1

Task: To examine my likes, skills, work experience, and aspirations
Objective: 1) To learn more about myself
            2) To develop self-confidence
            3) To find the sources of my satisfaction

Choose a time when you are relaxed and free to spend an hour or so on the following activity. It may be a bit harder to do than you expected. If you find it difficult to come up with more than a couple of short lists, take a break. Call a friend or relative and chat about what you're up to. Chances are they'll remind you of all kinds of things that will help you out.

Be thorough and remember, there are no right or wrong answers and nothing is too trivial to write down. If you already know exactly who you are and what you'd like to be doing, skim through the following and move on.

Part 1: What I like (would like) to do

On one sheet of paper, make a list of everything you like to do. Before you start, remember not to restrict your list to the obvious. You may be a salesperson in a clothing store, but may really prefer to design clothing. Only you know what you really like to do. Make sure you include things you've always wanted to do but never tried, such as scuba diving or race-car driving. Leave nothing out—no matter how personal—since only you need see this list.

 Entrepreneurs continually practice self-assessment

Part 2: What I'm good at

Using a separate sheet of paper, list what you are good at. Once again, don't restrict yourself to what you do at work (or what you did at work if you're now unemployed). For example, you may be a skilled machinist, but also be good at playing the piano. If you're a homemaker, don't overlook such skills as food and special menu preparation, sewing, building maintenance, child care, and so on.

Don't restrict yourself to activities that you think relate to jobs. Some of the most rewarding enterprises involve nontraditional forms of work. Look at your first list and see what you've learned to do as a result of your hobbies and outside interests. Do you collect stamps, postcards, or anything unusual? Are you an amateur expert on military hardware? Do you know every spoken line of script from every Humphrey Bogart movie? Take your time; be thorough. Leave nothing out.

Ask others what they think you're good at. You might be surprised. You may find out they think you're a great storyteller, or that you have a terrific eye for fashion. Your mother might say, "You know you've always loved to play the piano," or "When you were little you would build things with your Meccano set all day." If you have a job that entails regular reviews or evaluations, collect these and review them. Don't overlook your current job, no matter how familiar it seems. Whether you like it or not, you may well have developed useful abilities such as keyboarding, scheduling meetings, managing, and interviewing people. You may also have learned how to do a number of very specific tasks related to what your employer produces or sells. If you work in government, you may have learned a great deal about writing and assessing proposals, documents, and letters.

 Entrepreneurs consider all experience potentially useful

Part 3: What I do (did) for a living

Using a separate sheet of paper, list all the jobs you've had. If you've had more than one, list all the jobs you've had since you first started working for pay. Make sure you include part-time jobs and jobs you may have held for only a short time. If you've had only one job, this could be a very short list for you. If you're unemployed, write down what you did last. Circle the job you enjoyed the most. This may or may not be the job that paid the most money.   ▶ ▶ ▶ ▶▶▶▶

At the bottom of the list, write down all the reasons why you liked that particular job the most. Maybe it did, indeed, pay the most money or maybe it allowed you to walk to work instead of having to commute.

 Many entrepreneurs build new ventures on old jobs

Part 4: What I would like to do for a living

Using a separate sheet of paper, make a wish list. What kind of job would you really like to have? Don't exclude any occupation because it is too trivial to mention or because you don't think you possibly have a chance for such a job. Write them all down.

 Entrepreneurs aim high

Part 5: Analyzing your lists

Compare your four lists, setting them side by side so you can see how they relate to each other. Here's how they might look:

WHAT I LIKE (WOULD LIKE) TO DO	WHAT I'M GOOD AT	WHAT I DO (DID) FOR A LIVING	WHAT I WOULD LIKE TO DO FOR A LIVING
read novels	cooking	reception desk	play sports
meet new	driving car	clerk	test cars
people	typing	office manager	be a TV star
cook	meeting people	waiter	run own
fix my car	taking charge	sales manager	business
have company	computers	chef	
over	playing tennis	camp counselor	
do my friends'	dancing	work with kids	
hair	babysitting	play sports	
run	teaching	TV host	
play tennis			
design new			
products			
talk			
go dancing			

What does this picture tell you?

The next step is to see how these lists relate to each other. Play with them for a while. Match random items from each list and see what picture they paint. If you reach any startling conclusions, write them down. Now look at the reasons you liked the circled job best. Are any of those reasons related to your likes in List 1, your abilities in List 2 and your dream jobs in List 4? In our example, there seems to be a strong interest in athletics, young people, and self-employment.

Now that you've looked at your interests, abilities, and experience, pick the description of yourself that matches who you really think you are or would like to be. Pretend you really are that person. Now look in the mirror. Tell yourself who you are. How does it feel?

Evaluation

Even though there are no right or wrong answers to the exercise you've just completed, you can still perform a meaningful self-evaluation. Remember the objectives of these exercises?

1) To learn more about myself
2) To develop self-confidence
3) To find the sources of my satisfaction

Do the following:

Check one in each statement below. Give yourself 4 marks for every (a) choice, 3 marks for every (b) choice, 2 marks for every (c) choice, and 1 mark for every (d) choice:

1. I learned
   (a) ☐ a great deal
   (b) ☐ quite a bit
   (c) ☐ a little
   (d) ☐ nothing about myself from this exercise.
2. After listing everything I'm good at, I feel
   (a) ☐ a great deal more self-confident
   (b) ☐ quite a bit more self-confident
   (c) ☐ a little more self-confident
   (d) ☐ about as self-confident as before.
3. I am now
   (a) ☐ much better able
   (b) ☐ quite a bit more able
   (c) ☐ a bit more able
   (d) ☐ about as able as before
to describe what really makes me happy or gives me the greatest satisfaction.

If you gave yourself 12 marks, congratulations! Your self-confidence and self-knowledge will serve you well as an entrepreneur. If you scored 3, you probably were self-confident and self-aware when you started this exercise. But it's not the score that really matters. It's whether you see the point of the exercise and recognize the importance of the objectives.

⚷ KEY POINT Entrepreneurs crave feedback

Remember, the primary object of the exercise is to learn about yourself, not to change yourself immediately. You'll learn more about entrepreneurs and yourself as you read more of this chapter.

Where's the Money?

In the exercise just completed, you may have noticed that the question of which job paid the most, or had the most prestige, was not given much attention. That's because entrepreneurship is less about money than it is about pursuing your own personal goals. Money can be a great short-term motivator, but along with prestige and other superficial incentives, it will not take you the distance. That sounds like blasphemy, but it's a common misconception that entrepreneurs are money-hungry. Actually, entrepreneurs are achievement-hungry, and money is a necessary tool to that end. The next profile will help you understand this point.

PRO FILE

Entrepreneur: Peter Dalglish

Enterprise: Street Kids International

When Peter Dalglish graduated from law school, he was on the fast-track to success. As a lawyer he would likely have made a good deal of money, but something happened that sidetracked his legal career. It was 1984, the year of the great famine in Ethiopia, and Peter decided to help with the relief efforts. He was so shaken by the tragic plight of so many starving children that he decided to work full-time to do something to help.

Peter was in Khartoum, the capital of Sudan, working with street children, most of whom were completely destitute and had to resort to stealing to survive. He felt that the traditional way of helping—providing money or food—wasn't working. It was merely a short-term solution to a long-term problem. He was determined to find a better way.

"I asked myself, what useful skills do these kids have that they could use to earn a living? Well, the kids knew every building in the city—since they had broken into many of them—and I thought, why not start a bicycle courier service? Let's put the kids on bicycles and have them deliver mail and

parcels around the city. But run it like a business, not a charity. One of the problems was that the kids were illiterate and couldn't read the addresses on the envelopes. But children are very innovative and what they did was color-code their parcels. Many of the deliveries were to embassies and embassies have flags so the kids colored the parcels to match the flags.

"It didn't take long before the kids realized that it made more sense to learn how to read. But these kids couldn't go to school because they couldn't afford the mandatory uniforms, so they hired their own teachers with their own money and paid these teachers to teach them to read. The ones who learned how to read made more money."

The success of Peter Dalglish's Street Kids International is now well known and Peter continues to head the organization in spite of the fact that he makes very little money at it. But Peter learned early in life that money isn't everything.

"I have never been poor. I come from a well-to-do family and went to the best schools. And I learned at an early age that money does not equal success, or happiness. There has to be much much more than that. If success to you means the exotic vacations and the BMW then you are wasting your life. There can be nothing worse than lying on your deathbed knowing that you've wasted your life."

Peter Dalglish needs and uses money. He spends a great deal of time raising money to finance projects to help the millions of desperate children around the world. But he gets his satisfaction from the achievement of goals, not from the accumulation of wealth.

 Most entrepreneurs are not motivated by money alone

Putting money in its place

If you are tied to a wage or salary, with little control over your income, you might tend to see more money as the solution to all your problems. Money, after all, is an easy and obvious thing to wish for. Do you wish you had a windfall of cash?

What would you do with a lot of money? Why not make a wish list? Imagine you have just won a million dollars and fill out the following:

Wish list

If I had a million dollars I would _____

_____

_____

_____

Wasn't that fun? Spending a million dollars probably really would be fun, but take a look at your "What I like to do" activity. How would your million-dollar fantasy affect your true source of happiness, that which gives you your greatest satisfaction? If there is no connection between what will make you happy and having a huge sum of money, maybe you're just wishing for money without giving it much thought.

A closer look at the effects of instant wealth may reveal little that would actually raise your personal happiness quotient. Hackneyed as it sounds, material possessions can make life more comfortable, they can be amusing and fun but—for most people—they do not bring happiness. There is always a flashier car, bigger house, or more expensive toy to buy. Let money be the welcome by-product, rather than the goal of your enterprise. From that perspective it can do only good. When money is accumulated gradually, almost inadvertently, you have the time to learn how to manage it well. We give our children gradual increases in their allowances as they learn how to manage money effectively. As adults, most of us can manage $25,000 to $50,000 per year quite easily; $200,000 is another story, and a million is a big leap into the unknown. If this seems off-putting, relax. If money is part of your dream, you will get it. But, be aware that it's not your best long-term motivator.

To Dream the Possible Dream

If you are going to devote all your time and energy to a venture that may take years to bring to maturity, you need to be highly motivated. You will need to be totally committed to your venture, to persist against all obstacles to achieve your goals. Where will this motivation, commitment, and persistence come from? It will spring from the venture itself. You will be committed, motivated, and persistent because your venture will be a part of you; it will be uniquely yours.

You have dreams. You'll find them listed under "What I like to do" and "What I would like to do for a living." Daydream about them. Picture yourself achieving each one. In time, you will actively pursue a dream. It will be your venture and you will believe in your dream as only you can. You will pursue it doggedly through times when money and help are scarce; when your friends tell you to give it up; when your parents tell you to get a real job. When you've already worked seven 18-hour days, you'll put in seven more. This you will not do for money or for prestige. This you will do only for yourself — to fulfill your dream and prove to yourself that you can achieve it. That helps explain why:

 Entrepreneurs are motivated by a desire to achieve personal goals

and...

 Entrepreneurs are persistent

Total commitment

To be a successful entrepreneur, you have to be totally committed to your venture. If you are not truly bonded to your venture in a deep and meaningful way, or if you're only in it because you think it will be a good way to get rich quickly, you'll likely quit long before that happens. It helps to be intrinsically interested in what you are trying to accomplish.

Learning from hobbies

Do you have a hobby? Stop and think about how many hours you spend on your hobby. Do you count them? Or do you work at your hobby as long as you possibly can without paying any attention to the time? What motivates you to spend hours and even days doing repetitive tasks that most people might consider boring? Only you know. You are doing something you enjoy.

You set goals ("I'll assemble this model plane") and objectives ("Today I'll complete the tail section") and then you set out to achieve those goals and objectives. You have a vision of the completed task and when you achieve it you experience unique personal satisfaction. You aren't being paid for this and it's possible that no one will appreciate your achievement except you. The next time you're involved in your hobby, whatever it is, remind yourself that you're now as close as you can get to feeling like an entrepreneur.

 Entrepreneurs often build ventures on their interests

The Thrill of Adventure

There are more traits associated with the entrepreneurial character. You may already have some of them and you may develop others. You don't need all of them to the same degree, but you should know that all are in evidence when entrepreneurs are studied. One of the easiest traits to recognize is self-confidence. Where do these entrepreneurs get the nerve to do the things they do?

Entrepreneurs are adventurers. In fact, the word "adventure" means "to venture." The explorers of history were entrepreneurs. They used the latest knowledge of geography and navigation as a basis for their visions of great riches and opportunities beyond the known horizon. Determined and persistent, they championed their ventures from conception to completion, all the while risking fortune, reputation, life, and limb. Their efforts laid the economic foundation upon which we now all stand. You will be one of the new adventurers. Through your vision, skills, creativity, and innovation—your entrepreneurship—you will advance the frontiers of knowledge and achievement. In the process you will participate in laying the foundation for our economic future. All you need is the confidence to get started.

Developing self-confidence

You may already be an adventurer in someone else's eyes. Do you ski, ride horses, or travel to exotic countries? To someone who hasn't tried any of these activities, you might seem to be quite a daredevil! Take skiing, for example. As you plunge down an icy slope, you seem to be courting danger. But all you feel is exhilaration, not fear. That's because you have a great deal of experience and sharp, well-developed skills. But remember that you worked your way to this slope gradually. You wouldn't have had the confidence to try an expert run on your first day. As your skills improved, so did your confidence.

Entrepreneurship works the same way. You'll start on a "beginner slope," with a small, manageable venture. As you practice your entrepreneurial skills, your confidence to take on bigger ventures will grow.

 Entrepreneurs are self-confident adventurers

Taking risks: Rediscovering your childhood

No doubt you enjoy the thrill of adventure; most of us do. As a young person you probably rode roller coasters and did wheelies on your bike. You likely loved to explore caves and look under rocks. Where has that sense of adventure and curiosity gone? What happened? Where did that fearless self-confidence, that willingness to take risks go?

Likely it was sent into hiding as you worked your way through school. Too often, our education systems appear to discourage risk taking and new ways of doing things. It is said that children are born risk-takers. They start life full of self-confidence but then have it beaten out of them before they become adults. They enter school as question marks and leave as periods.

You can become an adventurous risk-taker again. If that frightens you a bit, that's good. Believe it or not, entrepreneurs generally don't like to take risks. They take risks because their dreams, curiosity, and need to achieve require that they do. To an entrepreneur the best risk is no risk—a sure thing. But, like betting on the favorite at the racetrack, a sure thing returns very little reward and often is not so sure after all. Often, entrepreneurs appear to be taking considerable risks when, from their perspective, they are very much in control.

Harold Warner is a good example of entrepreneurial risk taking. To many people he appears to be a major risk-taker and, indeed, Harold sees himself as something of an adventurer:

> "I have been down white-water rivers in canoes, been a poor bronc rider and been a race-car driver. I've never been too shy to try something, but I'm not a major risk-taker. In fact, I'm truly a coward in many respects, but if I'm intrigued by something, I'm not going to let life pass me by without trying it."

You'd be tempted to think that hanging in a wicker basket from a sack of hot air suspended high above the ground would be the biggest risk in Harold's life. Not so. Harold and his pilots are all highly trained and licensed to meet international standards of safety and performance. It may seem risky to you, but you may not be aware of the factors in play, and how they're controlled. Harold's risk is quite real, but it is more mundane than the risk to life and limb. He risks his payroll on the weather. In poor weather his balloons can't fly at all. He can't control the weather...or can he?

16

Risk taking and gambling

Do you like to gamble? Do you find yourself drawn to casinos to try for the big win or do you just plunk two dollars down for a lottery ticket from time to time and hope your lucky number will be drawn? Does this make you a risk-taker? You bet it does. Your chance of collecting on a lottery ticket is virtually zero, so you've risked your two dollars about as much as is humanly possible. Does it mean you are preparing yourself for the life of an entrepreneur? Not exactly.

You have likely guessed why by now. Control. Entrepreneurs are rarely gamblers because gamblers rely on chance to succeed, and chance is uncontrollable. Remember, entrepreneurs want to be in control. They take risks only when they have to, and then they try to minimize these risks as much as possible.

Managing risk: The risk-reward continuum

As an entrepreneur you will work with what is called a risk-reward continuum. In simple terms, the higher the risk, the greater the reward, and the lower the risk, the smaller the reward. Gambling is a high-risk pursuit with the potential for great rewards. If the future of a venture depends on it, you will not likely bet on the toss of a coin or the turn of the dice. However, once you have developed your own abilities, you will bet on **them**.

The next time you are in a gambling casino, take the time to look around and think about the casino as a venture. The odds always favor the house. Those are the odds an entrepreneur likes. The owner of the casino is betting only that gamblers will try to beat the odds—and lose. Given that gamblers rely on luck, the owner's bet is quite safe. The truth is that a casino is really selling entertainment in the form of gambling while its customers, equipped only with luck, are trying to avoid paying. There are likely entrepreneurs in the casino where you're gambling. They own the place.

You might think the entrepreneur is taking a big risk that every customer could win at once and the place would go broke. But the owner understands gambling, gamblers, and odds. He or she has managed the risk. As a gambler, are you managing your risk? You are if you went gambling as an entertainment, prepared to lose. Entrepreneurs may gamble for fun, but they would never gamble on their venture without taking every precaution and reducing every risk.

 Entrepreneurs are rarely gamblers

Risk and confidence—the upward spiral

Gambling is addictive. If you win, you want to win more. If you lose, you want to keep playing until you win, and so on. Entrepreneurship is addictive, too. When you take a chance on your abilities and ideas and win, you will want to keep on winning. Up goes the self-confidence. Although you try not to lose, sometimes you will fall short of your goals. But, by then you will know how to reduce your risks—you'll learn, practice, fine-tune your enterprises, and make an amazing discovery: Failure is as useful as success. Because failure can teach you valuable lessons about how not to do something, it increases your chance of ultimate success. The light bulb was not invented on the first try. Thomas Edison is reported to have said, "I now know a thousand ways to make a light bulb that will not work."

 To entrepreneurs, failure is an opportunity to learn valuable lessons

Armed with the knowledge of what you did wrong the first (or second, or twelfth) time, you will be more confident than ever on your next try. Even failure can increase your self-confidence. It's a win-win situation.

In pursuit of your dream, getting there is half the fun

You've likely heard it said in another context, but the old saying "Pursuit is sweeter than capture" is quite true when applied to your entrepreneurial venture. You will discover that, as much as you look forward to achieving your goals, your real satisfaction will come from pursuing your venture. You will become addicted to entrepreneurship itself. The very act of pursuing a venture is a continuous reward. Each day will present its own challenges and problems that you will meet and solve. Each small battle won will bring a jolt of satisfaction, charging you up to continue the quest. Long-term success will be a bonus, and failure will not daunt you. Enterprise, success, and failure will all feed your self-confidence and elevate your self-worth.

> Harold Warner says:
> "When I see my balloons, especially the neat shapes that I helped design, floating up over a city, it's as if my ideas are being floated for everyone to see. It's the greatest feeling on earth."

By the way, how does Harold control the weather?

> "Well, it may be raining in Calgary, and it may be windy in Denver, but it can't be raining and windy all over the earth all the time. So what we do is have as many different locations to fly our balloons as possible—Tokyo, Brussels, Montreal, or wherever. There has to be good weather somewhere."

If you still feel cautious about taking risks, you're already more like an entrepreneur than you might think. You will be ready to take more risks when you learn more about your venture. Each new step will bolster your self-confidence. But it wouldn't hurt to start with an act of faith.

Managing Your Beliefs

It's important that you believe in yourself. No matter what you think of yourself, there is no one anywhere like you. You are unique. Your thoughts are uniquely yours. By linking your enterprise to your person, you create a unique enterprise.

 Entrepreneurs believe in themselves

While you're working on believing in yourself, take some time to examine your personal set of beliefs. Everybody has one. What are your beliefs? You may be holding beliefs that conflict with your goals. This can create confusion and can significantly reduce your ability to achieve. It's not easy to list your beliefs, but it's worth trying because they play a significant part in how you approach day-to-day life.

EXERCISE 2

Task: To examine my beliefs
Objectives: 1) To learn more about myself
             2) To pinpoint conflicting beliefs
             3) To develop my entrepreneurial character

Listing your beliefs is a very private activity and only you will know how well you're doing at it. Here's an activity that might help you get started. Without thinking too much, put a check beside the statements that strike you as true:

1. People never change _____
2. Heredity is the main reason for success _____
3. Rich people are usually happier than poor people _____
4. I have changed a lot since I grew up _____
5. Success comes from working hard _____
6. You have to be lucky to be a success _____
7. Anyone can achieve their goals if they try hard enough _____
8. I will never be happy _____
9. Everything has already been invented or tried _____
10. There are fewer opportunities now than when my parents were my age _____
11. I can do less and less as I get older _____
12. Instinct is the best guide _____
13. Most successful people are dishonest _____

▶ ▶ ▶ ▶▶▶▶▶

14. Poor people are usually happier than rich people _____
15. Age is no barrier to success _____
16. You make your own breaks _____
17. We are all products of our environment _____
18. I cannot match the power of fate _____
19. As soon as someone gets a little, someone else takes it away_____
20. Everything is possible _____
21. I can do a lot, but I can't change my horoscope_____
22. There's no fool like an old fool_____
23. There's no such thing as a sure thing_____
24. Luck comes in streaks _____
25. Failure is evidence of a weak character _____
26. At the age of five you've learned most of what you will learn_____
27. You never stop learning _____
28. I have no control over my destiny_____
29. Caution is always the best policy_____
30. The best way to start is to jump in _____
31. I am in charge of my own fate _____
32. If someone else can do it, so can I _____
33. Experience is the only reliable teacher _____
34. Astrology is bunk_____

Evaluation

Go back over the list and see if some of these beliefs overlap or conflict. For example, if you checked 6 and 16, you believe in luck and yet you don't. Which is it? If you believe you can succeed, on the one hand, but on the other believe that only dishonest people succeed, you may find part of you dragging your feet as you venture forth. If you hold two or more contradictory beliefs, it's a sign that you need to take a hard look at your whole belief system.

Like most people you probably accumulate and absorb beliefs with more or less care and awareness. Once established, a belief can be a difficult tenant to evict. By listing your beliefs you lift them to the surface of your consciousness, where they will be exposed to reality. You may not be able to change them or discard them readily—indeed, you may not want to rid yourself of any of them. But you will at least know which beliefs are operating in your psyche. Over time, valid beliefs will grow stronger and invalid beliefs will evaporate. Of course, you are the ultimate judge of what is a valid belief for you.

Myth: The Entrepreneur As Loner

With all the previous emphasis on you—your skills, your control, your beliefs, and your dreams—you can be forgiven if, like so many people, you think that entrepreneurs work alone to achieve their solitary goals. As an entrepreneur, you will indeed be in charge of your venture and you will often feel very much alone, but you won't accomplish much without the help of other people.

As much as you might like to, you just can't do everything yourself and the sooner you learn how to put together a team and delegate responsibilities, the better. Look at it this way. You will want your venture to succeed so when you come up against a challenge that exceeds your own skills, you likely won't have the time to stop and learn the new skills yourself. Instead, you'll find the most skilled person you can for that task and you'll stick to doing what only you can do.

When you start out, you may be reluctant to share any of your future success. You'll learn that part of something is better than all of nothing, and nothing is probably what you'll have if you go it alone. Control has limits. You'll need financial partners and they will be concerned about the security of their investment. They'll want to be assured that your talents and skills are complemented as much as possible by the team you have assembled. In Chapter 2 you'll learn more about developing your team-building skills.

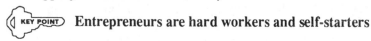 **Entrepreneurs are not loners; they are team builders**

Being your own boss

If you are primarily motivated by the chance to be your own boss, you'd better know what that means. It doesn't mean coming to work whenever you feel like it, taking long holidays, and power-tripping with your employees.

Entrepreneurship is hard work. Some entrepreneurs have been known to work seven days a week for years before taking a break. Most work much longer hours for themselves than they ever did for another employer. If you thought that having your own business would provide you with instant money and plenty of free time, please don't quit your day job!

If you are your own boss, why would you work yourself so hard? One reason may be that you have yet to learn how to balance your work and leisure time. Another overriding reason is that in the relentless pursuit of your dream, you won't be keeping track of hours and lunch breaks. You will move from task to task, problem to problem, and solution to solution without stopping to think about time, and you won't even think of it as work.

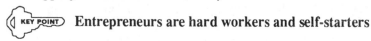 **Entrepreneurs are hard workers and self-starters**

Positive Thinking

Would you describe yourself as an optimist or a pessimist? Is this glass half-empty or half-full?

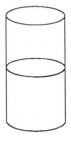

21

You might say that the positive thinker is grateful to have some water rather than none. Actually, entrepreneurs are more positive than that. They see the half glass of water as an opportunity to be filled. Entrepreneurs tend to see the shortage of something as a need waiting to be satisfied.

You'll have many more chances to practice this kind of positive thinking when you work on learning how to recognize opportunities. The only good to come out of moaning and complaining about the status quo is that it helps entrepreneurs to recognize opportunities.

Besides, as an entrepreneur you can't afford to waste time thinking in negative terms. You put a positive twist on every bump and pitfall. If one of your team members quits, you see an opportunity to find someone better. If business is slow, you take the valuable time to rework your strategic plan. If your venture goes bankrupt, you take the opportunity to put your new skills and ideas to work on the other opportunities you've had on hold.

 Entrepreneurs are positive thinkers

Inventors or innovators?

One common myth is that entrepreneurs are inventors and vice versa. In fact, inventors seldom make good entrepreneurs. Inventors like to tinker until their invention is just about perfect. They rarely think realistically about marketing their invention because they tend to assume that the perfect invention, like the better mousetrap, will attract buyers automatically. Entrepreneurs know better.

But entrepreneurs need inventors because entrepreneurs are innovators. Innovation involves putting an invention to use—possibly in a way the inventor never expected. For example, television wasn't designed to become a computer screen and microwave ovens were in use in restaurants for 20 years before someone decided to adapt them for the home market. The fax machine is based on technology that's more than 60 years old—in fact, faxes have been around for decades. It took an entrepreneur to adapt and distribute them for everyday use.

In Chapter 4 we'll look at innovation in detail. For now, remember that you don't have to be an inventor to be an entrepreneur. If you already are an inventor, you can still be an entrepreneur, but these roles are quite different. Although they are complementary activities, they require different skills.

 Entrepreneurs are innovators rather than inventors

Honesty: The Best Policy

Innovation often requires creativity, which is a skill most entrepreneurs sharpen and use daily. Do you imagine that entrepreneurs are creative in less-than-admirable ways—ways that reflect questionable moral and ethical practices? Do you intend to do unto others before they can do unto you? It's true that the practice of entrepreneurship is not restricted to those who work within community standards of business and social ethics. There are many unethical entrepreneurs in the world.

As you learn more about what entrepreneurs do, you'll see that certain criminals are skilled entrepreneurs. Unfortunately, the risk-reward continuum is often stretched to the breaking point in their cases. Prison has been home for more than one entrepreneur who failed to learn an important lesson: in entrepreneurship, honesty is by far the best policy.

Here's a quick quiz that will help you check your own ethics.

EXERCISE 3

Task: To review my entrepreneurial ethics
Objectives: 1) To learn more about myself
　　　　　　　2) To compare my ethics with those of most entrepreneurs

Your personal ethics are more complicated and far-reaching than this exercise will indicate. This exercise is merely designed to point you in some potentially useful directions as you continue to define and refine your own code of behavior.

Part 1

Imagine you are pursuing a restaurant venture. Answer "yes" or "no" to the following questions:
1. If your regular supplier sends you the shipment you ordered, but accidentally undercharges you, would you keep silent about the mistake? _____
2. You have a chance to buy a cheap shipment of meat that has not been properly inspected. If it looks and smells okay, would you buy it and use it? _____
3. When you hire new staff, do you first pick those with whom you might like to have a sexual relationship?_____
4. You discover an excellent, very inexpensive location for your new restaurant but it sits on land that might be polluted from a now-defunct factory. If you could bribe the authorities to forgo an environmental assessment, would you? _____
5. Your nephew needs a job and you owe his father a favor. Would you fire a loyal, experienced employee and give your nephew the job? _____
6. You're losing your shirt and a friend offers to burn down your restaurant so you can collect the insurance. Would you do it if it were virtually certain you'd never be caught? _____

Part 2

Check the comments that reflect your beliefs:
1. It's all right to do something illegal if you can get away with it._____
2. Everybody else is doing it, so to be competitive I have to, even if it's not right. _____

3. Cheating is part of the game. ____
4. By and large, honest people are suckers. ____
5. Big business is totally corrupt, so why should I be different? ____
6. There's no such thing as an honest buck. ____
7. Sometimes you need to make people do unnecessary things just to show them who's the boss.____
8. Only suckers pay taxes. ____
9. Everybody has a price. ____
10. What the customers don't know won't hurt them.____

Evaluation

If you answered "no" to the first six questions and checked none of the 10 comments, you're on the right track regarding entrepreneurial ethics.

Entrepreneurs may be among the most free individuals in our society, but they are bound by laws and customs, like everyone else. Questionable environmental, labor, health, and business practices increase risks, rather than reduce them. It makes good sense to stay away from avoidable problems.

Honesty makes sense

There's another, even more practical reason to be ethical. Whatever your venture, you will pursue it within a definable arena. Soon you'll discover that everybody knows everybody in that field of business. If you don't pay your suppliers properly, everyone will know. If you abuse your staff, everyone will know. You will reap what you sow. No doubt, even some dishonest people are forced at least to act honestly because of the day-to-day pressures of business.

 Most entrepreneurs are honest and reputable people

The following exercises will help you review this chapter while you assess your progress toward becoming an entrepreneur.

EXERCISE 4

Task: To evaluate myself
Objectives: 1) To review the characteristics common to most entrepreneurs
2) To compare myself with those characteristics
3) To highlight my strengths and weaknesses in order to develop and augment them

Circle the number that corresponds to how you would describe your entrepreneurial character and attributes. Put a box around the number that corresponds to how you would like to see yourself.

	(NOT AT ALL)			(TO A GREAT DEGREE)	
I'm persistent	1	2	3	4	5
I'm self-confident	1	2	3	4	5
I'm a self-starter	1	2	3	4	5
I'm honest	1	2	3	4	5
I'm hard-working	1	2	3	4	5
I'm goal-oriented	1	2	3	4	5
I like to try new things	1	2	3	4	5
I like challenges	1	2	3	4	5
I learn from failure	1	2	3	4	5
I feel good about myself	1	2	3	4	5
I take calculated risks	1	2	3	4	5
I am adventurous	1	2	3	4	5
I think positively	1	2	3	4	5
I learn from experience	1	2	3	4	5
I aim high	1	2	3	4	5
I have dreams of success	1	2	3	4	5
I crave feedback	1	2	3	4	5
I believe in myself	1	2	3	4	5
I love life	1	2	3	4	5

Evaluation

Successful entrepreneurs tend to have developed these characteristics to a great degree. If you circled mostly 4s and 5s, you are already well prepared to meet the challenges of pursuing a venture. However, if you're like most people, you likely circled a few lower numbers. Flag the characteristics you checked with a 3 or lower. You'll need to develop and strengthen them as you work through this book. But, don't let a few lower scores stop you from getting started. Most entrepreneurs develop many of these character traits "in the heat of the battle," as it were. If you circled all 5s, turn to the next chapter now!

EXERCISE 5

Task: To identify five entrepreneurs and talk to them
Objectives: 1) To explore the entrepreneurial character further
2) To compare myself with real entrepreneurs
3) To introduce myself to the environment of the entrepreneur

You don't have to do a formal interview with the entrepreneurs you've targeted. Just give them a call or drop in and say you're interested in what they do and want to know more about why they do it. The easiest and simplest way to do this is to make a practice of talking to the owners of businesses you normally use. Try looking for people who:
- started, own, and run a business
- introduced an innovative product or service in your community
- identified a real need in your community and set about filling it
- completely reworked an existing business and made it grow
- tried an old idea in a new way and made it work. ▶ ▶ ▶ ▶▶▶▶

Try to include one or two franchise owners. Some people think of franchisees as entrepreneurs, while others don't. Draw your own conclusions. Include in your research the owner of a local fast-food outlet, for example. Other suggestions: contractors, such as painters, builders, landscapers, and other tradespeople; real estate developers; child-care and senior-care workers; automobile dealers and manufacturers, if there are any near you. Don't overlook people who are clearly innovative and entrepreneurial just because they don't fit a preconceived category. You may know some entrepreneurs disguised as clergy, doctors, lawyers, civil servants, teenagers, athletic coaches, or community workers.

Remember, many entrepreneurs don't want their competition to know details of their ventures, so they might shy away from certain subjects, at least until they get to know you better. Don't press sensitive points.

Because entrepreneurs often love to talk about what they do, you may find a few of them willing to take the time to give you a half-hour interview. If you do, the interview guide at the back of the book may help you organize your questions and the information you will gather. Even if you just make a point of chatting about the same kinds of things with each entrepreneur, you'll be able to compare any trends that evolve.

Evaluation

The point of this exercise is to find out what entrepreneurs are like firsthand. The more you find out for yourself, the better. Did you find that the entrepreneurs you met matched what you've read so far? If not, how did they differ? Did talking to entrepreneurs increase or lessen your desire to be your own boss?

Some additional activities

Becoming an entrepreneur will change your perspective on life. To get started, you will have to do some changing, too. Here are a few simple activities that can help.

Try doing everyday things differently

Do two things to break your daily routine. Go for a walk after dinner; ask your children to set the agenda for a whole Saturday; take an entrepreneur to lunch; start a hobby that has always interested you; accept a leadership position that has been offered to you by a church group, social club, or service organization.

Feed your brain

- Read at least two different newspapers every other day. If you tend to read certain sections and skip others, make a point of reading sections you usually skip.
- Do you like to read magazines and trade journals? Try reading or scanning one completely different magazine or journal each week. For example, if you usually read newsmagazines, go to the library and browse through a cooking magazine or a computer magazine.

- There are a number of television programs that deal with business and entrepreneurship. Try to watch one or two each week.

In the next chapter you'll learn about the importance of developing skills that are important to entrepreneurship. Following is a summary of key points from Chapter 1.

 Summary

Entrepreneurs know who they are
Entrepreneurs see themselves as the product of their choices
Entrepreneurs continually practice self-assessment
Entrepreneurs consider all experience potentially useful
Many entrepreneurs build new ventures on old jobs
Entrepreneurs aim high
Entrepreneurs crave feedback
Most entrepreneurs are not motivated by money alone
Entrepreneurs are motivated by a desire to achieve personal goals
Entrepreneurs are persistent
Entrepreneurs often build ventures on their interests
Entrepreneurs are self-confident adventurers
Entrepreneurs are rarely gamblers
To entrepreneurs, failure is an opportunity to learn valuable lessons
Entrepreneurs believe in themselves
Entrepreneurs are not loners; they are team builders
Entrepreneurs are hard workers and self-starters
Entrepreneurs are positive thinkers
Entrepreneurs are innovators rather than inventors
Most entrepreneurs are honest and reputable people

2 Upgrading Your Skills and Knowledge

Like anything else, it's not so hard—once you know how to do it.

❧ EVERYBODY WHO KNOWS HOW TO DO SOMETHING YOU CAN'T

Do you know how to swallow swords or eat fire? Do you ever wonder how hard it is to fly a jetliner or drive a racing car? Have you ever asked a musician how long it takes to learn to play the guitar, or a ballet dancer how she or he achieved such grace and poise? If you're like most people, you've often wondered what it takes to do things you think are exciting, dangerous, or amazing. The answers to these questions can be either encouraging or discouraging, depending on how much you learned in the first chapter.

If you believe that such deeds are beyond ordinary human capability, you may think you have a good excuse for not attempting them. But, if you are now developing the confidence to believe that your dreams are within reach, you will be encouraged by the answers to the questions above.

There is no magic. No superhuman skills are required. Although natural talent plays a part in all human endeavors, exotic skills and jobs are no different from any other. Musicians, ballet dancers, jet pilots, and fire-eaters will tell you that to do what they do you simply have to do what they did: **Learn, practice, and work hard for a long time.** In this chapter, you'll learn:

- how to assess and use specific skills you already have developed
- how to discover forgotten skills
- about general skills that most entrepreneurs share, such as team building, financial management, research, marketing, and goal setting, and how you can develop them
- how to organize your network
- how to communicate clearly
- the importance of marketing.

Skills are the tools entrepreneurs use to build their ventures

The Importance of Skills

Since you want to become an entrepreneur, you'll have to learn the skills that entrepreneurs use.

General skills, which are shared by all entrepreneurs, include communication, team building, and financial management skills. Specific skills relate to your particular venture. For example, if you're planning to start an innovative cleaning service you'll need to know as much as possible about cleaning.

PRO FILE

Entrepreneur: Alva Atkinson

Enterprise: Nightingale Computer Cleaning Services, Ltd.

Most people don't like to do cleaning, which is why so many cleaning services compete to do the job for them. At one time, Alva Atkinson could barely afford food and shelter, let alone a cleaning service. She was a divorced mother of three children, on welfare and desperate to do better.

When she landed a job with a company that cleaned offices, she noticed that, although they cleaned the phones, nobody ever cleaned the computers—and it showed! It was too risky, they said. Computers are mysterious things, they said. Better left alone.

Those answers didn't satisfy Alva Atkinson. Somebody must clean computers, she reasoned, and she was going to find out how they did it. It made sense that the companies who manufactured the computers should know, so Alva approached a large manufacturer who happily explained the process. She learned quickly. All it took was care, the right cleaning materials and some basic cleaning skills. She quit her job and started looking for a contract of her own.

"I knew that many companies used computers," Alva explains, "but I quickly figured out that there was one industry that has used lots of them for longer than just about any other—newspaper publishers!" Alva landed her first contract with a major newspaper and Nightingale Computer Cleaning Services was launched.

Alva has never looked back. She personally trains her employees—as many as 14 when times are good—and she revels in the financial freedom her company has given her.

"After two years I took my children to Disneyworld for three weeks, and paid cash for the whole holiday. It was a good feeling."

Tools of entrepreneurship

In Chapter 1 you reviewed some of the things you're good at. You probably discovered that you have more skills than you might have thought. These skills are your entrepreneurial tools. Just as each entrepreneur is unique, each has his or her own set of tools.

It's time to take a more detailed look in your skills tool box. In the following exercise you'll identify and list some specific skills you've acquired either at work or home.

EXERCISE 6

Task: To list and rate my specific skills
Objective: To make sure I know what I can do

Part 1

Here are a couple of sample lists to illustrate how to itemize your skills. Using them as an example, create your own list of skills, based on your experience. Check off to what degree you have acquired these skills.

Carpenter

I AM ABLE TO: (LEVEL OF COMPETENCE)

	BEGINNER	SOME EXPERIENCE	EXPERT
identify types of wood			✔
identify quality of wood		✔	
relate type to cost		✔	
use circular saws			✔
estimate contracts	✔		

Shift supervisor

I AM ABLE TO:

	BEGINNER	SOME EXPERIENCE	EXPERT
organize schedules		✔	
assign tasks to others		✔	
prepare reports	✔		
do inventory		✔	
train new people	✔		✔

My current occupation

I AM ABLE TO: (LEVEL OF COMPETENCE)

	BEGINNER	SOME EXPERIENCE	EXPERT
_____	____	____	____
_____	____	____	____
_____	____	____	____
_____	____	____	____
_____	____	____	____
_____	____	____	____
_____	____	____	____
_____	____	____	____
_____	____	____	____
_____	____	____	____
_____	____	____	____
_____	____	____	____

Evaluation

As you worked through the lists, were you surprised at the number of skills you've developed? This exercise can be a great confidence builder if, like most people, you've lost track of some of the things you've learned to do over the years.

Review your lists and pay particular attention to those skills you've developed to the expert level. You'll have a head start on your venture if you choose to identify an opportunity in an area in which you have expertise. For example, carpentry skills could help prepare you for a construction or manufacturing venture. You may not necessarily build your venture around the areas in which you are expert, but you will, almost certainly, have occasion to use all your expertise at one time or another and that will save you time and money. After this exercise, you should be better aware of what you're good at doing.

Finally, are there any skills that you want learn? Why? If your employer is insisting you learn them, why is that so? Are they really important and general skills, like keyboarding, or are they highly specific skills which are likely not applicable outside your current job? Pay particular attention to the skills you want to learn for your own reasons. Your desire to learn a skill could be a strong indicator of where you should look for opportunity, later on. For example, if you really want to learn how to do welding, you may find a venture related to metal fabrication.

▶ ▶ ▶ ▶▶▶▶▶

Part 2

If you've worked at one type of job for a long period of time, you might have forgotten whole sets of skills that you haven't used for awhile. It's easy to get into a mindset that allows you to think only of skills you've used on a paying job, when you may be skilled at all sorts of other things.

Hobbies are a good source of hidden skills. Do you play sports? If you do, you likely know quite a bit about the human body, kinetics, and how to hurt and heal yourself. You probably know lots about the sports you play—soccer, for example. Whatever your hobby or pastime—whether it's sailboarding or coin collecting—you have honed some very specific skills in pursuit of it. Write down your hobbies and list the skills you've acquired through them.

My hobbies

I AM ABLE TO: (LEVEL OF COMPETENCE)

	BEGINNER	SOME EXPERIENCE	EXPERT
_____	_____	_____	_____
_____	_____	_____	_____
_____	_____	_____	_____
_____	_____	_____	_____
_____	_____	_____	_____
_____	_____	_____	_____
_____	_____	_____	_____
_____	_____	_____	_____

Remember your roots

At one time, the best recommendation someone could bring to a new job was the experience of growing up on a farm. This often mystified the aspiring employee, but the reason was obvious to a prospective employer, who could guess that anyone with experience on a farm knew how to work hard and probably also knew how to:

- operate heavy equipment
- do minor or major repairs to equipment
- use tools effectively
- work with animals
- sow, nurture, and harvest crops
- handle and use chemicals
- do basic carpentry, plumbing, and electrical work
- drive cars and trucks
- react to medical emergencies
- work with ropes, knots, chains, and pulleys
- predict the weather and its effects on crops, animals, and soil
- adapt to climatic extremes.

If you grew up on a farm, or in a family that operated a business, or if you just had a paper route, think hard about what you learned as a result of that job or environment. Nothing is too trivial to list. Often the skills we take for granted most are among the most important in the long run.

My forgotten skills, job, or experience:

I WAS (AM) ABLE TO:	(LEVEL OF COMPETENCE)		
	BEGINNER	SOME EXPERIENCE	EXPERT
_____	_____	_____	_____
_____	_____	_____	_____
_____	_____	_____	_____
_____	_____	_____	_____
_____	_____	_____	_____
_____	_____	_____	_____
_____	_____	_____	_____
_____	_____	_____	_____
_____	_____	_____	_____
_____	_____	_____	_____

Evaluation

Are you surprised at how many skills you already have? Did you uncover any that you hadn't thought about in years? Did this exercise make you feel more capable and self-confident because you are more skilled than you thought? Or did this exercise make you realize that you have a lot to learn? Either way, you achieved the goal of the exercise, which is to find out what you can do and how well you can do it.

 Entrepreneurs know what they can and cannot do

Specific skills and knowledge

Skills and knowledge go together like peaches and cream. Take a look at the exercises you completed above and note all the entries in the "expert" or "some experience" column. To become expert at any skill you must have learned a great deal more than merely how to do it. If you are an expert at operating heavy equipment, for instance, you will know a lot about heavy equipment. It's not often thought of this way, but farm equipment is heavy equipment. It's not too hard to drive a farm tractor, but after years of operating one in a wide variety of circumstances, you will have learned a great deal about the machine itself. For example, you will likely know about:

- internal combustion engines and how they work
- hydraulic systems and how they work
- pneumatic tires, traction, and gear ratios
- pulley and driveshaft horsepower ratings
- transmissions and clutch systems
- cooling and lubrication systems
- metal types, strengths, and methods of repair
- indications of wear and strain
- fuel types, dangers, and handling techniques
- noise, fumes, and their effects on the operator
- performance in mud, on dry surfaces, or in snow
- brake systems and performance under specific loading conditions
- compatible equipment and relative performance ratios
- replacement value of the machine and its parts
- the origin of the machine and its manufacturer.

Although these skills may sound quite technical, people who grow up on farms often know all of the above, and more, by the time they are teenagers.

How did you learn to do what you do?

It's possible that you consider yourself a skilled driver, but you really know very little about the workings of internal combusion engines. You may have learned by rote. Do this, that happens. Do something else, something else happens. You have practical, but not theoretical, knowledge about driving. It's also possible that you know a great deal about cars, but can't drive one. In that case, you have theoretical, but not practical, knowledge of driving.

There are different ways of knowing things. You'll need to be honest with yourself about some of your skills. Maybe you know computers inside out, but you can't keyboard at even 20 words per minute. You're computer-literate, but you're not great at word processing. Try the next exercise.

EXERCISE 7

Task: To compare my practical and theoretical skills
Objective: To know what I know

Go back over all the lists you made in Exercise 6 and, for each skill listed, put one of the following codes beside it like this:

PT: I have both practical and theoretical knowledge of this skill

pT: have theoretical but little practical knowledge about it
Pt: I am quite skilled at doing this, but don't know a lot about it
pt: I have little practical or theoretical knowledge of this skill

Evaluation

By going over your lists, you should now see a more complete inventory of what you're able to do and how much you know about each skill. Some of these skills may need more practice; others may need more study. It depends on what you intend to do with them. In later chapters, after you've identified your venture, you'll be able to use these checklists to help you determine where you need to do the most work and on which skills. But for now, let's look at how well you've already developed some general skills, and how your specific skills relate to them.

General Entrepreneurial Skills

No matter what kind of venture you might plan to launch, you'll need some fundamental general skills, such as financial management, marketing, team building, and the like. Many entrepreneurs aren't good at all these skills, which is why it's important to develop your team-building skills—so you can work with others who complement your own strengths and weaknesses.

Teamwork

Ron Foxcroft is a highly skilled, extremely successful entrepreneur. Of all his skills, he ranks team building as the most important.

Entrepreneur: Ron Foxcroft

Enterprise: The Fox 40

"I was lousy in school," reveals Ron Foxcroft, "but I loved athletics." Ron's love of sports continued long after he left school. Even while he was building a successful trucking and warehousing business, he remained actively involved in basketball, where he's been a player, coach, and, in recent years, a referee.

Not one to do anything halfway, Ron became a professional basketball referee. But, in sport, as in business, he is particular about details. For example, other referees put up with the somewhat-imperfect pea-whistle that almost all referees in all sports use daily. But these whistles sometimes fail. If a referee blows the pea-whistle too hard—they call it overblowing—the little ball of cork (which long ago replaced the pea) jams, leaving the referee with a red face and a missed call.

Ron was officiating an Olympic basketball final match when his whistle jammed during a key play. He determined then and there that he would make a better whistle—one without a pea.

Success in business, as in team sports, depends on choosing the right player for the right job. As a referee, Ron knew how to blow a whistle, but he knew nothing about whistles in general. So when he set out to make a better whistle, he drew on his knowledge of team building to help him solve the problem. Since he's not an inventor, he hired an industrial designer to reinvent the whistle, a plastic injection-mold specialist to manufacture it, and a marketing specialist to sell it.

He matched the right person with the right job.

"From athletics I learned the value of teamwork. I get my greatest thrill from putting a team together and watching them get the job done," says Ron Foxcroft. Three years after he handed the challenge to his team, the Fox 40 whistle was a reality—and a huge success.

"It has no moving parts," Ron beams, "so you can't overblow it." Today, the Fox 40 whistle is the official whistle of the National Basketball Association and the National Football League. Millions have been sold world-wide and Ron Foxcroft, now millions richer himself, still officiates at basketball games. But his whistle never jams.

Team building can be applied to every enterprise. Ron used his general skill—his ability to build effective teams—to harness the specific skills of the members of his team. Are you an effective team builder?

You can't do it all yourself

Being a team player is different from being a team builder. Ron Foxcroft gave his team the responsibility to come up with a new whistle and a marketing plan to sell it. He built and led the team, but he wasn't a member of the team.

If entrepreneurs share a common fault, it's likely in the area of team building and delegating responsibility. "This is mine—all mine!" cry immature entrepreneurs. "Nobody understands my venture as well as I do, so I have to do everything myself. I just can't trust other people to do these critical tasks! I do all the work and I get all the money and all the glory!" Unfortunately, fledgling entrepreneurs like these will likely learn the hard way, not the smart way.

If you are a mature, skilled entrepreneur, you'll be focused on attaining your goal in the most efficient, practical way. You'll probably have a number of partners and investors who feel the same way. You'll know you need the best, most skilled person for each of the many jobs your venture will create and that you can't do all of them yourself.

 KEY POINT   **Entrepreneurs are skilled team builders**

How good are you at team building? Have you ever had to choose a crew to tackle a tough job? How did you do it? Did you choose your friends or did you choose the best people for the job? Of course, your friends might have been the most skilled people, but a good team builder considers many factors.

Be wary of the relative who does a little accounting

It's natural that you would first approach your family for advice about your venture. If you don't know much about financial management, for instance, your father might recommend that cousin Marvin who dabbled in accounting for awhile. Marvin could very likely be your first, big mistake. Remember, successful entrepreneurs always seek the best possible advice and the best possible people for the job. If Marvin doesn't qualify, tell dad and look elsewhere.

But look where? How do you find the right people? It really depends on a number of factors, especially the type of venture you're planning. Today, everybody specializes. If you're involved in a retail venture, you'll need people who know retail. You're likely better off hiring a low-profile accountant who really knows retail than a high-profile, expensive financial wizard who has never had anything to do with buying and selling.

Probably the best way to find people is by word of mouth. The recommendation of someone who has had at least as much to lose as you and whom you know and respect well may be worth more than the opinion of a stranger to you and your venture. In Chapter 1, I encouraged you to get out and meet some entrepreneurs. If you did that, you likely found someone you can relate to. Ask that person for recommendations.

Networking

Networking is a skill in itself, and it's a great way to find the people you need. You already have a network—you probably just don't think of it that way. Your network is everybody you contact on a regular basis—friends, relatives, and business associates.

Most people just let networks happen. When they meet people, they exchange business cards and say things like, "Good to have met you. Let's have lunch sometime," and leave it at that. When they need to contact that person, they search frantically through stacks of business cards and old notes, trying to find the right phone number. To build and use a network effectively, you have to work at it.

When you meet someone you want to keep in your network, file their name and number by what they do, or by a category that makes sense to you. Most importantly, know where to find them and when. You will quickly build a large network of dozens, perhaps hundreds of people. Make a point of contacting one or more people in your network every day. Staying in touch means staying in touch, not just calling in emergencies.

Get used to saying to yourself, "I wonder what Bill would think of this idea," or "I should ask Maria what she thinks of the new labor legislation," and then call those people. Remember, you are in their network, too. The more you stay in touch with them, the more you're part of their network.

EXERCISE 8

Task: To organize my network
Objective: To organize information about the people I know

In this exercise you will identify and classify all the people you already know into easily accessible categories.

If you already have some word-processing skills, you may want to set your network up on a computer. But if you're more comfortable with file cards, use them.

Whom should you include? Everybody. There's a reason you have someone's address in the first place, so if you had no good reason to discard it up to now, you should enter it. Include relatives, neighbors, teachers, co-workers, and, of course, businesspeople.

Start by gathering all your address books and the business cards you've already collected. Then work your way through them and arrange them according to the skills those people have. For example:

Financial management

Marguerite Langlois (Address; phone; fax)
- Bank manager   Notes: Arranged last loan. Got lower rates.
- Mortgage specialist
- Date last contacted: 07/07/9-

Giuseppe Travanti (Address; phone; fax)
- Chartered Accountant   Notes: Did income tax last year.
- Tax expert
- Date last contacted: 02/01/9-

Trades, construction

Sam Jennings (Address; phone; fax)
- Housing contractor   Notes: Built addition on my house.
- Experienced job estimator
- Date last contacted: 05/08/9-

Janis Smith (Address; phone; fax)
- Architect   Notes: Won award for recent work.
- Commercial buildings specialist
- Date last contacted: 03/21/9-

This will take some time to accomplish, but nothing is more important than beginning your network now. Once your venture is launched, you'll need quick access to all kinds of professionals, tradespeople, and just friends, who happen to be skilled at something you aren't skilled at.

It may take you days or even weeks to get your network up to date. You won't mind spending the time now if you realize that the right advice and help could save you months of unnecessary work later on.

If you're computer literate, you should use an address-book program. With most programs, you can get the computer to search for specific people or skills. You might command it to find a lawyer with experience in the food industry, for example. Your computer will deliver that information in a second. It's a simple step from there to moving all your information to mailing programs as you need it, for address labels, for example.

But you can't do any of this if you don't classify and enter the information in the first place. Don't get someone else to do it for you. Do it yourself. You probably need the review and you're the best judge of how to classify certain people. For example, you might have a teacher in your file who is an expert inventor, or a family friend who cooks as a hobby.

Evaluation

Networks are living things—always changing and growing. If your network is small, don't worry. Now that you're prepared to add to it, it will grow quickly. If you've just slaved for 10 days creating your database, you can be comforted with the knowledge that keeping the network up will be much easier from now on. Just add new business cards to a pile, along with any other records of a new acquaintance. Then, schedule an hour a week to update your file.

 Entrepreneurs are experts at networking

Communication: An Essential Skill

Networking will be one of your most valuable general skills, but it is just one of many. Just as networking will help you as a team builder, there is one skill that will help you with virtually all aspects of your venture—communication.

What is communication, anyway? Recall something in the past week that made you laugh or smile inwardly. Now tell someone else about the incident as accurately as possible.

There are many different ways to accomplish this. You could explain the incident verbally, draw or paint a picture, write a paragraph describing the incident, or you could re-enact the incident on the actual spot. After all that, how do you really know if you've succeeded? If the other person laughs just as you did, you've communicated well. But, if you have to keep retelling the story to get even a glimmer of a smile, your communication skills could use some sharpening.

To sell is to communicate

Before we get into identifying and improving your communications skills, let's take a look at why you need to do this in the first place. It's simple: few things will doom your venture more than your inability to sell it to others.

If you're like most people, you may tend to take offense at the notion that you aren't yet a skilled communicator. After all, you can read and write. You regularly carry on conversations with people and they seem satisfied. You might think that if the other person doesn't know what you're talking about it must be his or her own fault, because you think you're certainly explaining it clearly enough.

It won't matter much whose fault it was if your meetings, phone calls, and letters are fruitless. But the only way you can minimize the chance of failure is to make sure you're doing your part correctly.

It sounds complicated because it is complicated. A skilled communicator will make the process seem effortless. A poor communicator will struggle to transfer only a hazy approximation of the original idea. How do you rate as a communicator? When you give directions on how to travel somewhere, do people always have to ask you to clarify them, or give more details? When you explain something, do you find that people always seem to get it all wrong? These are signs indicating the need to improve your communications skills.

Most people learn how to talk well before they're five years old. But there's a difference between talking and communicating. Most of us need to improve our talking skills in order to communicate effectively. However, if you want to find out how well you can talk, try this exercise.

EXERCISE 9

Task: To listen to myself talk
Objective: To determine the need, if any, for improvement

Although it's not easy to talk about something off the cuff, you shouldn't have much difficulty talking about yourself without preparation.

Get a small, inexpensive tape recorder. Put in a clean tape, press the record button, sit back, and deliver a two-minute (or longer) oral résumé about yourself. Use the following questions as a guide:

- What is your name?
- Where are you from?
- Describe your education.
- Describe your most recent employment. What did you do? How did you like it?

Evaluation

Play back your presentation. What do you think? Are you surprised at how you sound? Do you hear annoying speech mannerisms, such as "uh," "like," or "umm"? Does your inflection rise at the end of each sentence or phrase, as if you're asking a question? Do you speak more slowly, or quickly, than you thought? Do you think the tape recorder must be faulty?

Some tips on improving your oral presentation:

- Be self-aware when you speak. Notice and remind yourself of things that annoy you.
- Think before you talk.
- Slow down. Use pauses. Vary your volume level.

Additional activity

Do all the above, using a video camera on a tripod. That way you can also study how you appear to others. Don't expect to look and sound like a network anchorperson on your first try. Professional announcers and television hosts take years to develop their skills. But, do keep trying and improving. Do both these exercises again after two or three months, and note your progress.

🔑 KEY POINT Entrepreneurs are generally good talkers

Eventually you'll develop your own unique way of communicating. Ron Foxcroft got his venture off the ground by being obnoxious—in a friendly kind of way.

Ron took his new Fox 40 whistle to the Pan-American games with the hope of attracting some interest from all the referees in attendance. After a couple of days he was discouraged because he just couldn't seem to get their attention.

One night he had an idea. "I'm talking," he thought, "but they just aren't listening. Maybe I ought to wake them up first." So he waited until about 2:30 in the morning. Then, armed with his whistle, he marched down the corridors of the dormitory where the referees were sleeping, blowing his whistle as he went. The piercing sound immediately woke every referee, and when they emerged from their rooms, none too pleased at the disruption, Ron said, "See, I told you this whistle works."

He came home from the games with orders for 20,000 whistles.

Know your audience

All communications are not equal. You talk and write differently to your mother than you do to a bank manager. However, it's your job to tailor your communications to the person who will be receiving them.

Put yourself in their shoes

Pretend you're going to meet a banker to try to borrow some money for your venture. Before you plan your pitch, consider the position all bankers start from: What's in it for the bank? You believe in your venture, and you believe your returns will be fabulous, but if you succeed, all the bank gets is the usual rate of interest. In other words, the upside is better for you, and the downside is bad for both of you.

Pretend you're the banker. You are supposed to loan money and collect interest. But you want to be as certain as possible that the loan will be repaid, and that it's secure if it isn't repaid. That means you'll want to see evidence of:

- a careful, detailed explanation of how this money will be spent
- a realistic explanation of how the money will be repaid
- useful collateral to cover the whole loan, or guarantees from third parties to that effect.

As the banker, you don't want to hear:

- vague, unrealistic, pie-in-the-sky descriptions
- rambling, disjointed explanations of financial details
- poor answers to simple questions.

And, you don't want to see:

- sloppy, handwritten information
- inappropriate dress and appearance
- a casual, devil-may-care attitude.

Finally, as a banker, you have only limited time, so you want all the information you need delivered quickly and efficiently and in language that you're familiar with.

Empathize

How did it feel to be a banker? The single most important skill you can have as a communicator is to be able to put yourself in the position of the people you're communicating with. The key word is empathy. If you know what it feels like to be the person you're talking or writing to, you'll know whether to:

- use simple or more technical language
- use humor or just stick to business
- speak quickly and get out or take your time and be thorough
- write in a familiar or neutral style
- use first names, surnames, or titles
- refer to a potentially sensitive incident or not
- use fire and passion or remain cool and detached
- hand over your business card with one hand or two (Asians use two).

If you're able to empathize with your listener, you will sense hesitation, nervousness, boredom, distraction, or genuine interest and you'll be able to adjust your presentation accordingly. If you're only halfway through and your listener is fidgeting, cut to the chase quickly. Have your material arranged so those options are available.

First impressions are very important. If your listener senses that you understand and appreciate his or her position, you will greatly increase the chances of a successful meeting, phone call, or letter.

Here are some tips to help you empathize:

- Consider the time of day, day of the week, and week of the year. People get tired at the end of the day, and anxious at the end of the week and just before holidays. Know when holidays occur for different cultures. You may not celebrate the Chinese New Year, Hanukkah, or Christmas, but your listener might.

- Arrive early for a meeting so you can learn little bits of information from the receptionist, or from printed material that might be lying about the waiting area. It helps if you can refer to something positive that just happened, like a jump in the company's stock or the completion of an important sale. But don't start something you can't finish.

- As your meeting starts, note personal details of your listener's office. If pictures of family members are prominently displayed, you may want to mention your own children or family, if that's appropriate. For example, "Your children appear to be about the same age as mine."

- If you haven't set a time limit on the meeting, ask how much time is available and try to use less. If your subject is happy to go over, acknowledge that as a bonus.

- Don't just talk, listen! Listening tells you about the other person. The more you know about the person you're communicating with, the more you can tailor your language and format to that person. Listening means using your eyes and brain as well as your ears. People communicate in many subtle ways, including facial expressions, gestures and the speed and tone of their language. Your listener might have said, "I'll look into this and get back to you," but how was it said? Was it used to get rid of you, or was it genuine?

- Acknowledge your listener's situation. If he or she suddenly takes a coughing fit or finds out that a loved one has been in a serious accident, back off. It wouldn't make much sense to try to finish your pitch anyway and you'll be seen as a caring, sensitive person, rather than a brute.

Meet the challenge

In summary, to communicate effectively, you have to adapt your communications to the person who's listening. If you speak at a college level to someone who is barely literate, that's your problem. If you are ignorant of someone's culture, language, and customs, that's your problem. If you have no idea how well you got your idea across, that's your problem. If your idea was completely misunderstood, that is truly your problem. You've seen how some of these problems can be avoided. Let's look at some other communication challenges you might face.

 Entrepreneurs study the targets of their communications

Phone Etiquette

We've already touched on face-to-face communications of the kind you'll use in a meeting, but there are many other media to carry your messages, including telephoning, faxing, and letter writing.

Although the computer has become a primary piece of business equipment, there is one business tool that is more important than all the rest put together—the telephone. Entrepreneurial innovation has generated hundreds of changes and improvements in the familiar device, but its basic purpose has not changed. The telephone allows you to talk to someone who is not near you.

Used effectively, the telephone will save you time and money. Used ineffectively, the telephone will frustrate you and those you're calling, and will cost you plenty in unnecessary trips and lost contacts.

The right tool for the job

You'll be using your phone often, so make sure that it's state of the art.

Speed dialing allows you to program numbers into your phone's memory so you need touch only one button to enter what can be a nine- or ten-digit number. Statistically, it takes three and one-half calls to actually complete a call to a businessperson, hence the logic of last-number-redial capability. Avoid speakerphones and never use them to carry on a conversation while you continue working at your desk. If you don't have time for the call, don't take it or make it!

If you plan to receive lots of long-distance calls, look into 800 numbers. If you plan to make lots of long-distance calls, there are many plans that can save you money. Talk to your local telephone company about your needs and make sure you get what you need, not what they say you need.

Telephone dos and don'ts

Here are some general rules for making and receiving telephone calls.

DO: Think about the call before you make it. Know what you want from this call and make sure it's worth knowing.

DON'T: Phone without a reason. Long distance costs add up, but even more importantly, people don't appreciate unnecessary phone calls.

They'll take you as a lightweight at best, and a fool at worst.

DO: Speak clearly and simply.

DON'T: Eat while you talk or talk too quickly.

DO: Use this format for an initial call: "Hello, this is.... I'm calling long distance (if true). I'd like to speak to.... Yes, I'll hold for a minute." If the person you want to speak with is unavailable, say, "Please tell...that I called and I'd appreciate it if he/she could return my call at his/her convenience. My number is 123-4567, and the hours of 9 to 5 are best for me. Thank you." If the person you want to speak with takes your call, say, "Hello, thank you for taking my call. My name is....I'm calling regarding...."

DON'T: Spend too much time talking to an operator or receptionist.

DO: Record the time of your call and any pertinent information, such as where the person might be the next time you wish to call.

DO: Return all calls. You can wait a day or longer, but do it. Successful entrepreneurs always return calls.

DON'T: Say "I'm sorry, I have to let you go. I have another call waiting."

DO: Say, "I'm sorry I can't talk any more right now. Perhaps I can call you again later."

DON'T: Waste your breath talking to someone who will only transfer you to someone else.

DO: Insist on talking to the person you asked for.

DO: Answer this way: "Hello, this is.... How may I help you?"

DON'T: Answer by saying, "Hello."

DO: Be considerate of the other person's long-distance costs when they call you.

DON'T: Remind a valued caller that you're paying the long-distance charge.

DO: Use good manners, regardless of the nature of the call.

DON'T: Ever hang up on anyone you may ever want to speak to again.

Follow these specific rules for business calls:

DO: Set up initial meetings by telephone.

DO: Call to confirm, if the meeting was arranged a long time in advance.

DO: Initiate calls personally whenever possible.

DON'T: Have someone else initiate a call for you unless it can't be avoided.

DO: Ask if your caller minds your use of the speakerphone.

DON'T: Surprise your caller by announcing: "You're on the speakerphone."

DO: Tell your caller who is in the room with you and why.

DO: Pay your telephone bills. You can't afford to lose your telephone.

Fax—Yes or No?

This part is simple. Buy a fax machine. Learn to use it. You'll need it to send or receive:

- prices or related financial quotes
- invoices
- letters that have to arrive as soon as possible
- sketches, photos, or anything difficult to describe in words.

In time you'll find you use your fax for all sorts of other communications as well, but try to:

- call ahead before sending your fax
- follow up with good-quality hard copy sent by mail
- avoid really long faxes, unless previously cleared
- avoid sending a fax when the message is not urgent. Use the mail.

Sometimes fax machines can make all the difference, as Terry Batson learned.

PRO FILE

Entrepreneur: Terry Batson

Enterprise: Batson Distributing

As an aspiring entrepreneur, Terry Batson found that being only 18 years of age was a liability. No one wanted to take him seriously. When he became interested in acquiring the distribution rights to a product manufactured in the Pacific Rim, he began doing all his negotiations by fax machine.

Terry is an articulate young man, so the manufacturer had no idea of his age. Soon Terry had acquired exclusive distribution rights for his whole country, and nonexclusive rights for a neighboring country. And the manufacturers never knew they had cut a deal with a teenager!

Get a Computer

If you don't yet know how to use a computer, what are you waiting for? A five-year-old child can be taught to create a file, type some characters and activate a printer in less than 15 minutes. As an adult, you may take a bit longer, so get started.

Although computers are used in virtually every sphere of human activity, the most common uses include word processing (writing), financial management (accounting), and CAD (computer-aided design). The simplest of these is word processing.

Word processing is what you used to call typing. Today, typing is called keyboarding and typewriters are now used as boat anchors and door stops. No doubt you've heard all the reasons why you should use a computer to write letters, résumés, and so on, and there's no use in beating you over the head with it here. But no matter what venture you undertake, your competitors will be using computers and this skill will give them a considerable advantage over you. So here are just a few words of advice, and then I'll leave the subject to you and your conscience.

The best advice is to acquire your computing skills in an ad hoc fashion. That means learn as you go. If you only need to know how to write letters, don't confuse yourself with learning how to do spreadsheets. No matter where you live, you will know someone who can do this. Take an hour, sit down with that person and just do it.

Written Communications

When you were in school you had a teacher to correct your writing for you. If you wrote poorly, you received a low grade. As an entrepreneur, you'll be writing to your customers and business associates. If you write poorly, you'll lose contracts and contacts. You can't let that happen.

First, the bad news: The rules of the game are simple and critical: Misspelled words, typographical errors, and incorrect language in general are not tolerated in serious business transactions. The good news: You don't necessarily have to go back to school to learn how to do it right.

Talking and writing are similar in that we tend to think we're better at both than we usually are. Talking is more dangerous because once you've said something, you can't stop, change it, and say it again without appearing unprepared at best, and just plain amateurish at worst. But cheer up, because when it comes to writing, all that matters is how your message appears when it's finally delivered. It doesn't matter how it got written, or who wrote it.

Here are three simple suggestions you can use from the very beginning:

1. Make sure that someone on your team knows how to write using proper business language.

2. Always have a second person review an important letter or document before it is sent.

3. Don't send handwritten letters to people you've never met.

Note the difference between the two letters on the next page.

The difference is that the letter on the right is a final draft, while the one

on the left is a rough draft. Never send a rough draft to anyone except an editor (and even then you might want to reconsider!)

 Entrepreneurs make sure it's right before it goes out the door

Communicating with Your Team

The most important communications you'll be involved in are often the most overlooked—communications among your own employees. Too often, entrepreneurs assume "everyone is clear about what we're doing, where we're going, and why." The results of this misguided assumption can be catastrophic.

Misinformation and mistrust soon take hold when people are left to figure out what's going on and why. They begin to presume evil intentions on your part because you seem to be keeping them in the dark. They talk among themselves and not to you. Soon you have a disgruntled and poorly motivated group on your hands and you don't know what happened.

What happened was that communications were allowed to flow randomly, like a mountain stream, instead of being controlled and shaped, like a canal. Make no mistake, there will be communication among your employees whether you control it or not. But without proper management, this communication will be based on hearsay, innuendo, and sometimes pure fantasy.

Entrepreneurs crave control and in attempting to keep control they sometimes fail to keep their employees properly informed. "Information is a matter of 'need to know,'" they like to say.

But employees and team members need to know, too. They want to feel part of the process, part of the inside group. You have to trust them with information. In short, you have to trust them with power. Done right, this will make you even more effective, as your employees will pull together rather than going off at cross-purposes.

Lines of communication

It's not difficult to set up proper lines of communication once you recognize the importance of doing it.

Schedule regular meetings with specific purposes and keep to the schedule. Nothing is more important than keeping those dates. The meetings can be short, but have them. Memos are okay and bulletin boards serve a purpose, but nothing replaces regular meetings. Discuss:

• plans for growth (where you are and where you should be)

• works-in-progress (who's doing what and why)

• general business.

And by the way, communication is not another word for manipulation. No matter how subtle you think you are at manipulating ("Say, Joe, I think you're really good at selling, so I'm going to move you up and take a bite out of Jane's territory"), you will be transparent to someone. In communication, as in life, be honest!

An entrepreneur in the communications field, hoping to impress her employees with her willingness to tighten her belt, announced that she was taking a 20% pay cut. She seemed a bit surprised to see her employees were unimpressed. What she didn't know was that, according to the rumor mill, everyone thought she had been paying herself $250,000 a year, which meant her salary would be cut to $200,000—big deal! In fact, she was cutting her salary from $100,000 to $80,000. If she had simply told them how much she was making in the first place, they would have likely applauded her honesty and sacrifice.

Here are some simple don'ts to be aware of when communicating with your team:

1. Don't expect your employees to share your dream; they have their own dreams. If you play it right, they may include your venture in their dream.

2. Don't expect them to be excited about making you rich; they're more interested in making themselves some money.

3. Don't assume your employees know what's going on.

4. Don't assume no one will want to know; they will.

5. Don't assume that because you've explained something, everyone will understand it, remember it, or care.

6. Don't keep closed books. It's risky, but the new way of doing things is to open your books. If you want loyalty, you'll have to pay for it.

7. Don't assume anything. Ever. Except taxes.

KEY POINT **Communication is the lifeline of entrepreneurship**

Communication is tremendously important. But you can always improve. The most important quality you can bring to improving your communications skills is humility. If you don't think you need to learn, you're not likely to learn much.

Learning how to learn, how to research, and how to organize are closely related activities. They all involve setting priorities and then dealing with them systematically.

Informal Learning

If you thought your learning days were over when you completed formal schooling, you're wrong. Learning never stops. You learned all kinds of things today, but what were they? How can you use this knowledge? If you can't answer those questions, it's because you aren't aware of the learning process and that's because you aren't consciously controlling it.

No doubt you often say, "I didn't know that before!" But learning is too important to leave to chance. You have to direct it.

On a day-to-day basis the simplest way to learn is to be self-aware and observant. Expect to learn things. When things go wrong, ask yourself, "Why did that happen?" and then look for an reason. If your day seems to be careening out of control, stop and ask what is causing this. If you find you don't understand a phrase in a book, ask someone what it means. When your mechanic tells you the "remostrad" is shot in your car, ask him or her to explain what a remostrad is, and why it's important.

If you're afraid of filling your head with useless information, don't be. There is no known upper limit when it comes to storing information in your brain. Lower limits are more common and more dangerous.

Your place of work is a classroom

Although you've already looked at what you might have learned at jobs you've had in the past, it's time to take a look at what you can learn in the job you have right now. No job is too insignificant.

High school students will often say, "Boy, I wish somebody would pay me to go to school!" Later, after school they add, "What a lousy job this is, working in the doughnut shop! I wish it paid better!" Too bad they think school ends at 3:30 p.m. If you have a job in a doughnut shop, think of it as being paid to go to school. If you bother to think and observe, your job can teach you:

• how to mix ingredients, set temperatures, and cook doughnuts
• how to work with complex equipment
• what customers expect from a doughnut shop and how to please them
• which products sell well or don't sell well and why
• how to operate a cash register, make change, and balance a day's receipts
• health regulations related to selling food to the public
• how decor, colors, and seating arrangements affect sales
• how to manage waste
• how to order just the right amounts of raw materials
• how to display the product so people will want to buy it
• how to communicate with customers in a professional way
• how to hold your tongue
• the importance of economies of scale
• the importance of test-marketing a product
• what franchise royalties are and why they're paid
• the meaning of product liability
• what bosses or managers do, and why
• how much money a doughnut franchise might gross in a day or year
• what kinds of people frequent doughnut shops
• how to manage and secure a commercial building
• how alarm systems work
• how to deal with thieves
• how to make the most of low wages
• how employees are promoted and why
• the difference a location makes to a doughnut franchise

- the cost of operating a franchise and the net profit
- about shrinkage and its relation to profits
- how to manage time responsibly
- something about every doughnut shop in the world.

All this, and you get paid, too! You can help the process along by asking questions, getting involved, and asking to do different types of tasks within your company.

Do you know what everyone else does at work? Why not find out? When you have spare time, get someone to teach you how to use the computer. Have the accountant show you what accounting system she's using. Ask your boss for information on the franchise or corporation that owns your company. Have lunch with someone of a different nationality and take informal language lessons from them. Now, **you** think of things you can start learning at work.

PRO FILE

Entrepreneur: Kaaydah Schatten

Enterprise: The Ceiling Doctor

Kaaydah Schatten was born into a poverty-stricken alcoholic family. One day she asked a farmer for some money. The farmer said, "I'll tell you what I'll do. I'll advance you some eggs, which you can sell and you can earn some money." It was her first entrepreneurial experience, at age seven.

Kaaydah was diagnosed as dyslexic, but that didn't stop her from learning. She used tapes and memorized books, making use of her fantastic memory. Tragedy struck when, at the age of 17, she was involved in a serious accident which left her paralyzed. Although she was told she would never walk again, she re-learned that skill and, using the insurance money from the accident, she bought a duplex. She decided to renovate the duplex, turn it into a four-plex, and then sell it, but she didn't know anything about real estate.

Kaaydah simply offered to work for a real estate company for free, much to the amazement of the realtor. After a year, she felt she had learned enough and promptly launched into a frenzy of real estate activity, amassing $5 million by the time she was 21.

The boom went bust and Kaaydah lost almost all her assets. But she had learned even more than most people. She learned that when it comes to renovations, the messiest job is removing and cleaning industrial ceiling tiles. So when she quit real estate, she decided to develop and launch a ceiling tile cleaning service which would clean tiles in place, with no removal necessary. Kaaydah researched and developed her own patented, innovative process, which employs biodegradable chemicals.

> Kaaydah designed The Ceiling Doctor as a franchisable company from the outset, and today spends most of her time selling franchises to key partners in targeted countries around the world.
>
> As of 1993, Kaaydah's company, The Ceiling Doctor, operates nearly 150 franchises throughout the world, but Kaaydah's still not satisfied. "I've had enough dirt floors. I don't want to be just a millionaire," she says. "I want to be a billionaire."

 Entrepreneurs never miss an opportunity to learn

Formal learning

The age of lifelong learning is upon us. Courses and programs of learning are springing up like mushrooms all around us. In a commercial district in one North American city, more than 10 private learning centers could be counted within three city blocks! Government-sponsored retraining programs are jammed with eager clients, many of them gray-haired, who are keenly aware of what life has to offer those whose skills have been rendered obsolete.

As an entrepreneur, it's not likely you'll need formal diplomas and degrees. What you will need are knowledge and many varied skills. Once you know which venture you want to undertake, you can go back over your lists of skills and knowledge in this chapter and identify the areas you most need to develop. Then you can find formal programs that can teach you these skills. Often colleges will allow you to audit a course, without credit for less than the cost of a credit course and without having to write any papers. You can attend as you are able and learn only what you need.

If you were a poor student in your youth, don't despair. Many entrepreneurs did not do well in school. But all made up for it when they began their ventures.

Schooling is easier the second time around

You'll find learning can be a lot of fun—especially if you haven't taken a course in a while. Here's how to upgrade your skills and knowledge with formal education.

1. First find out what learning facilities are located nearby. Go to the nearest school or public library and find out what colleges or high schools are offering courses for your age group and degree of experience. Send each a letter, or phone them, asking for an outline of courses offered at their institutions.

53

2. Review the course offerings and note the ones that interest you. Before spending valuable time and money on a course, arrange to meet the instructor to make sure the course will be what you hope it will be.

3. Many small businesses with progressive management will pay for upgrading your education and skills. If you work for a large corporation, check to see what training programs are available through their organization. You may be able to pick up computer, keyboarding, or accounting skills this way.

How to do research

It's possible that you can do all the research you need just by asking a few people on the street what they think of your new product. But it's not very likely. Research will mean the difference between success and failure for your venture, so you have to know how to go about it.

The easiest way is also the most expensive. Hire a professional researcher or market analyst who already has the skills. For many people this is the best route to take, since becoming a good researcher takes time. You can find this kind of professional help under "Consultants" in your phone book, or through your financial adviser.

But there are ways to shorten the process and narrow the field. If you live near a college or other institute of higher learning, pay a visit to its business studies department. It's likely that they can steer you to the kind of research you need, or possibly even do it for you. In some cases, you might interest a graduate student in including your research in his or her studies.

For example, you may wish to introduce a new food for export. Among your many research requirements, you'll need to know which countries would use it, what their import restrictions are, if any, and how much it would cost to ship the product to them. You might get some of your information from the government—a department of international trade. Other information could be gleaned from other businesses who are not in competition with your product. Still more information might come from the consulates or embassies of the countries you've selected for export.

Sometimes entrepreneurs are so convinced that they're onto a good thing that they just don't want to hear evidence to the contrary. "This is a sure thing!" they cry. "No need for research. It'll just be a waste of money." Research is never a waste of money, unless it's spent trying to prove that black is white. You'll need to know that your market really does exist, that you can produce your product at the price and quality necessary, and that you can deliver it on time and in quantity. To know this requires research.

 Entrepreneurs use only the best research for the task at hand

Marketing

Without research you won't get far at anything, especially marketing. You'll need lots of research to develop a marketing strategy, but you'll need to know something about marketing first. Marketing is a key skill that you or someone on your team must know well. But, you should at least be familiar with the basics of marketing and why it's important.

In its simplest form, marketing drives advertising and promotion. It determines who will buy the product and what those customers are like, where they live, where they shop, and how they can be most effectively reached.

One of the reasons inventors often don't do as well as experienced entrepreneurs is that they don't know how to sell and don't really appreciate how important selling is. They sometimes assume the product will sell itself. It won't. That's one reason why inventors need entrepreneurs—to sell their inventions.

Some people think that good selling makes up for a bad product, but nothing could be further from the truth. Even if you invented a cure for the common cold, people would not beat a path to your door. You'd still have to sell it.

That's where research and marketing skills come in. You have to know whom you're selling to, and be very clear about what you're selling. For example, others may think you're selling a document-shredding service but, to your clients, you're selling security, and to the tax department, you're a manufacturer of shredded paper.

Most entrepreneurs have a fairly good sense of their market: who their customers are, their age, sex, income bracket, and why they're potential customers in the first place. If you don't, hire a market research company to find out for you. You need this information. You also need to know how to get your particular customers' attention. Never assume it will be easy.

Know your customers

The key to marketing is knowing what you're selling and to whom. With that knowledge you can develop the right kind of marketing strategy for your market. For example, you'd use a different strategy to sell something to teenagers than to new parents. You'll get to know your market when you do a proper evaluation of both your opportunity and your idea later on. For now, it's important to know the relative importance of marketing to the overall success of your venture.

Under-promoting is one of the most common marketing mistakes; another is overlooking the obvious. Russ Parker didn't miss on either point.

PRO FILE

Entrepreneur: Russ Parker

Enterprise: The Calgary Cannons

If you're a sometime baseball fan who tunes in for the World Series, you may not know about the Calgary Cannons. The Cannons are something of a phenomenon in the Triple A League—that's just one notch below the Big Leagues. In the few short years since Russ Parker picked up the franchise, the Cannons have become one of the most viable franchises in Triple A.

The reason is marketing. From the beginning, Russ Parker realized he would have to work hard to fill the stadium in a city that already had professional football and hockey teams. So, for training and advice, he decided to turn, not to other baseball franchises, but to Disneyworld. He studied how the Disney people market their events and he adapted their techniques to baseball. He invented his own version of family entertainment—an evening with the Calgary Cannons.

When you go to a Calgary Cannons game, you know from the moment you clear the turnstiles that you're into something different from the usual sporting event.

Every game is an event, all right, but sports is only one part of it. Each game is a special occasion, whether it's kids' night, tropical shirts night (complete with steel bands), or the night a couple got married, right on the pitcher's mound. During one change of innings, a pizza delivery person appears, yelling "Who ordered the pizza?" Those who yell the loudest "WE DID!" have the pizza thrown in their direction, to the delight of all. When the Cannons score a run, a real cannon fires a hearty "BOOM!" The refreshment peddlers are trained, Disney-style, and, in the spirit of the game, throw change back to customers inside a hollow rubber ball. In short, when the crowd leaves a Cannons game, they may not know who won, but they, and the whole family, had a great time.

Russ Parker isn't selling baseball—he's selling entertainment, to the hilt. Like most successful entrepreneurs he knows how to walk a fine line between under- and over-exposure. Over-exposure isn't a problem for many people. In fact, most entrepreneurs don't promote enough.

To get your message across you have to expose people to it; put it in front of them over and over again. The old adages, "It doesn't matter whether people love you or hate you as long as they know your name" and "There's no such thing as bad advertising" contain more than a few kernels of truth. The hardest hurdle to overcome is getting your customers' attention. Even if you've run your promo a thousand times, it's new to anyone who hasn't seen or heard it before; and it's reinforced in those who have seen it more than they care to.

The power of advertising

You won't learn marketing overnight, but it is crucial to your venture. If you need a reason to believe in its importance—especially when it comes to shelling out hard-earned cash for it—look around you. Do you really think all those other entrepreneurs would spend the money they do on advertising and promoting if they didn't have to? If you don't yet have the marketing skills of a pro, or if you don't have access to a good marketing person for your team, the easiest policy to follow is to study your competition. If you're aiming at the same market, you'd be wise to go a similar route.

If you're just starting a video rental service, for example, and your product or service is much like someone else's, the safest way to market it is to copy your competition. It's not innovative and it won't make you particularly entrepreneurial, but you will learn about marketing, advertising, and promoting videos.

When they advertise, your competition is really giving you all kinds of marketing research. Study their ads and you can quickly figure out whether they're aiming at teenagers, adults, or senior citizens. You can tell by the ad: the music, the ages of the actors, and the time of day it appears on radio or television. Teenagers tend to stay up late, while older folks tend to go to bed earlier.

Once you know the game a bit, you'll have to be more innovative to set yourself apart from everybody else, just as Russ Parker did.

Marketing tips

Here are some tips to help you learn more about marketing without taking special courses (which are the best way of all, if you have the time and money).

- When you see an innovative campaign, talk to the promoters about it. Ask them how it works, how much it costs, where they got the idea, and what the drawbacks are, if any. Examples of this might be billboard promotions for roadside attractions ("Will the groundhog see its shadow? Be here on Groundhog Day!") or advertising toiletries in public washrooms.

- If you're not a professional graphic artist, do not design your own logo, sign, or business card. It will likely look unprofessional and possibly downright silly. People study and practice for years to get good at that kind of work. Pay them to do it right. How many customers are worth the few hundred dollars a classy logo will cost? You won't have to re-do it later, either. Besides, your competition likely hired a professional, not an amateur, and they wouldn't have spent the money unless they had to.

- Test your strategy before committing to it. It costs far less to re-do a prototype, or mock-up, than it does to undo a full-blown campaign. If you know your market, but haven't tested anything before, hire someone who has. It's that simple and that important. Products that sell well in one country, for instance, may bomb in another, even if it's presumed to be similar. A well-known cake-mix company, for example, thought the British would like extra-moist cakes because Americans do. Well, the British happen to prefer drier cakes, and somebody ought to have known that. One simple market test would have saved thousands of dollars.

You'll learn about venture plans in Chapter 5, and part of your plan will include your marketing strategy. You'll need to spell out: what you're selling, to whom (age, gender, income bracket), the size of your potential market, which advertising media you'll use (TV, radio, print, direct mail), your advertising budget, and much more. But, to do any of this, you'll need to be organized.

Organizational Skills

What does your bedroom look like? If it resembles an explosion in a laundromat, your office will look just like it. Do you regularly forget to take a vital piece of paper or article of clothing or spare tire with you? Are you always searching for a pen, paper, or a phone number? Do you assign two people to the same task without realizing it? Are bill collectors knocking on your door even though you have sufficient money to pay your bills? If any or all of the above ring true for you, you are disorganized and you will have to change to be an effective entrepreneur.

If you're like many of us, you envy organized people. You may even resent them for it. "How do they do it?" you may ask yourself.

Fortunately there are a few simple techniques we can easily learn that will allow us to look those other people squarely in the eye. Check each of the following:

- Purchase and use a daily planner. Enter all information regarding meetings and appointments—phone numbers, addresses, and the like.

- Use a short mental checklist before leaving home every day. Stop at the door and ask yourself: Do I have my briefcase? Check the planner. Where am I going? What will I need when I get there? Do I need to have any other phone numbers, names, or addresses? Can I accomplish anything else while I'm in that neighborhood?

- Make a habit of refueling your car when you are not in a rush, doing your laundry before you go away on business, and doing all your filing at the end of the day or, at least, every week.

- Use little notes to yourself. (Post-it notes work well.) Place them near the door, so they won't be missed: "Turn on answering machine," "Let out cat," "Get milk." Others that help can be put in the bathroom: "Get haircut," "See doctor," and so on. Your house may end up looking like a bulletin board, but these things really do work.

And soon your habits will change, and you won't need all those crutches.

 Entrepreneurs are organized—either by choice or necessity

Balancing the books

Although it's true that entrepreneurship isn't just about money, it isn't not about money either. You don't have to be an accountant to succeed as an entrepreneur, but you will have to develop a healthy respect for the bottom line—and the numbers that show profit or loss—and how to find it. Entrepreneurs often love to delude themselves into thinking they're better off than they really are. Accountants are dedicated to preventing and curing that potentially fatal disease.

Generally speaking, accountants will not advise you to spend money, but will rather provide a wall of arguments as to why you should not spend money. Entrepreneurs need this kind of advice.

If you don't know anything about money management, do two things right now:

1. Take a course in basic financial management. There are a lot of these courses available these days, so you may have to shop around for the one that's best for you. Ask your accountant, if you already have one, for tips on what to study and where.

2. If you don't already have a good accountant/financial manager for your venture team, start looking for one now. Use your network to help you find the right person for your needs. If you have a venture backer— someone who is helping finance your venture—that person will often suggest a particular person or firm. Be careful here, as there are unscrupulous people out there waiting to fleece someone who is unable to read a spreadsheet. But, find someone, because you won't make it out of the starting blocks without this skill or knowledge, whether it's yours or someone else's.

 Entrepreneurs always know where the bottom line is

Setting Goals

The following apocryphal tale has been handed down from entrepreneur to entrepreneur.

Walking through the woods one day, a young entrepreneur noticed a large tree with a target painted on it. As she drew closer, she noticed an arrow stuck precisely in the center of the bull's-eye. Realizing she might be in the line of fire, she glanced around anxiously to see who had fired this amazing shot. At first, she couldn't see anyone, but soon she noticed an archer in a faraway clearing.

She was so taken by the archer's incredible accuracy that she rushed up to meet him. As she approached, he was casually inspecting his bow, seemingly unimpressed with his own skill.

"Did you do that?" she asked.

"I did, indeed," replied the archer.

"But how could you, at such a distance?" she continued, her voice full of awe.

"Actually, it was quite easy. I'll show you." And with that, the archer leaned back and fired another arrow far into the distance. He then picked up a small bag and said, "Follow me."

Together they trudged off in the direction of the arrow's flight and soon they found it, stuck in a perfectly ordinary tree. The puzzled young entrepreneur watched and then laughed as the archer removed two cans of paint from his bag and casually painted a target around the arrow. "Fools 'em every time," he commented.

If you aim at nothing, you'll hit it every time

Like this fictional archer, many of us don't bother to choose clear targets in life. We fire our efforts in haphazard directions and then try to make sense of what we hit. In essence, we're painting the target around our arrows. When you use this method, you're always starting over and never improving your aim.

Like archery, goal setting is a skill. You don't have to hit the bull's-eye every time, but you do have to aim at a clear target. The trick is to set achievable goals and to raise your standards as you improve. If you start by trying to hit a small target, hundreds of steps away, you'll quickly lose confidence as you fail miserably.

Keep that challenge as your ultimate goal, but start by aiming at a large, close target. You'll likely be hitting the bull's-eye with ease before long, and you'll confidently move the target farther and farther away. When you do manage to score a bull's-eye it won't be a fluke or a trick; you will have earned your victory. Better yet, you'll have enjoyed a whole series of confidence-building accomplishments along the way.

There's an old saying that goes, "Every long journey begins with the first step." Right now you're on a long journey to become an entrepreneur. You've already taken the first few short steps.

When you think of goals your mind probably starts to swim. So many possibilities, so many different types of goals, so far to go, so much to do. You're not alone in your confusion. Until we impose some order on this chaos, we're all at sea. First you have to categorize your goals.

For example, we all have goals related to our personal lives. You probably have career goals, too. But some of your goals are more like objectives, or short-term goals, and some are things you hope to accomplish during your lifetime. Let's take a look at how to set short- and long-term goals. I've used the example of someone who wants to learn keyboarding, and I've included helpful comments. Later on, in Exercise 12, you'll get to practice setting your own goals.

EXERCISE 10

Task: To look at how to set long- and short-term goals
Objective: To think about your own goal-setting skills

Long-term goal:	To keyboard at 60 words per minute (wpm)
Short-term goal:	To find a course in keyboarding
	This is a start, but when will you achieve 60 wpm? Next week? Next year? Try to be more specific.
Long-term goal:	To keyboard at 60 wpm within one year
Short-term goal:	To enroll in a keyboarding course within two weeks
	Better, but why not set some intermediate goals and qualify your short-term goal a bit more?
Long-term goal:	To keyboard at 60 wpm within one year
Short-term goal:	To enroll in a keyboarding course within two weeks
Intermediate goal:	To complete the keyboarding course
	Your goals are becoming clearer. Now you need a strategy to achieve them and a system of evaluation to measure your progress.
Long-term goal:	To keyboard at 60 wpm within one year
Strategy:	To complete a keyboarding course and to use this skill in all my writing
Evaluation:	Course completed? Note wpm on a monthly basis
Intermediate goal:	To complete the keyboarding course
Strategy:	Attend every class, do homework, practice
Evaluation:	Course completed? _____
	Grade attained? _____
	Satisfied with your progress? _____
Short-term goal:	To enroll in a keyboarding course within two weeks
Strategy:	Phone schools to inquire; ask friends who have the skill; enroll
Evaluation:	After two weeks, if not enrolled, why not? _____

Be realistic

We're all familiar with vague and unrealistic goals, such as: "Someday I'm going to lose weight." Our strategies are just as impressive: "One of these days, I'm going to go on a diet." As long as today isn't "one of these days," I won't have to worry about missing the target.

When you set your goals, be realistic and clear about when and how. Instead of saying, "Someday I'm going to lose weight by going on a diet," try, "I'm going to lose five pounds over the next month by cutting out all desserts." You see the difference?

Whenever possible, be positive

The example above is negative. To accomplish your goal you have to lose weight, by going on a diet, which means cutting out desserts. Why not set a different goal that will accomplish the same thing? "Starting today, I'm going to start living a more healthy lifestyle by eating more nutritious foods and by taking up an active sport."

 KEY POINT **Entrepreneurs set positive goals: "I will" rather than "I won't"**

The following exercises will help you list and evaluate your general skills. When you've identified those that need particular work, do the exercise on goal setting at the end to help you get started on improving them.

EXERCISE 11

Task: To rate my general skills
Objective: To know where I have to improve

Complete the following checklist. For each skill, or set of subskills, check the evaluation that represents your current ability. For each of those skills that you want to improve, write "achievable" in the blank under "Expert." For those skills that you think you'll never be good at, write "delegate," indicating you'll need to find someone to do this for you.

SKILL	BEGINNER	SOME EXPERIENCE	EXPERT
Team building	_____	_____	_____
Networking	_____	_____	_____
Communication:	_____	_____	_____
telephone	_____	_____	_____
fax	_____	_____	_____
word processing	_____	_____	_____
writing	_____	_____	_____

SKILL	BEGINNER	SOME EXPERIENCE	EXPERT
Research	_____	_____	_____
Marketing	_____	_____	_____
Advertising/promotion	_____	_____	_____
Organization	_____	_____	_____
Financial management	_____	_____	_____
Goal setting	_____	_____	_____

Evaluation

Summarize your strengths and weaknesses by listing them. Where would you fit in your own team? Which tasks would you have to delegate? If you're lacking in some key areas and unlikely to develop these skills to any degree, you must consider those factors when you decide on a venture. A communications venture, such as video production or special events presentations, wouldn't be a good choice if your writing and speaking skills are poor and aren't going to improve. Remember these skills when you're assessing your window of opportunity later on.

EXERCISE 12

Task: To practice setting goals
Objectives: 1) to organize and focus my various goals
2) To develop a strategy for improving my skills

Make a list of all the skills you've identified by the end of Exercise 6 on page 33 as being achievable. Using the grid below as a guide, develop long-term, intermediate, and short-term goals (both business and personal ones) and a strategy for achieving them. Remember to set achievable goals with clear time limits on how long it will take you to achieve them. State how and how often you will evaluate yourself. Use Exercise 10 as a guide.

Skill: _____

Long-term goal: _____

   Strategy: _____

Intermediate goal: _____

   Strategy: _____

   Evaluation: _____

Short-term goal: _____

   Strategy: _____

   Evaluation: _____

▶ ▶ ▶ ▶▶▶▶▶

Make copies of this chart and use them to set long-term, intermediate, and short-term personal and business goals.

Before turning to the next chapter to find out how to spot opportunities, here's a summary of the key points from Chapter 2.

 Summary

> Skills are the tools entrepreneurs use to build their ventures
> Entrepreneurs know what they can and cannot do
> Entrepreneurs are skilled team builders
> Entrepreneurs are experts at networking
> Entrepreneurs are generally good talkers
> Entrepreneurs study the targets of their communications
> Entrepreneurs make sure it's right before it goes out
>   the door
> Communication is the lifeline of entrepreneurship
> Entrepreneurs never miss an opportunity to learn
> Entrepreneurs use only the best research for the task
>   at hand
> Entrepreneurs are organized—either by choice or necessity
> Entrepreneurs always know where the bottom line is
> Entrepreneurs set positive goals: "I will" rather than
>   "I won't"

The New Golden Age of Opportunity

"Though fortune be blind, it is not invisible."

&# Sir Francis Bacon

Some people despair that all the great opportunities have already been exploited, and that anything worth doing has already been done. They're wrong.

Sometimes it seems that the entrepreneurs who became so successful just happened to be in the right place at the right time and—bingo! It looks like luck, but chance actually plays a much smaller part in success than most people think. The key to success lies in learning to recognize and evaluate opportunities. In this chapter, you'll learn:

- how to recognize opportunities in needs, wants, and challenges
- how problems can be opportunities in disguise
- why entrepreneurs welcome change
- how to take advantage of technological and societal change
- how to spot trends
- how to discover niche markets
- how to evaluate opportunities.

First, meet an entrepreneur who has mastered the art of identifying opportunities.

PRO FILE

Entrepreneur: Les Hulicsko

Enterprises: Riteway Manufacturing, Riteway Cleaning and Sweeprite

When he was a young man in Hungary, Les Hulicsko graduated with a degree in mechanical engineering. But his engineering career was cut short when he found himself embroiled in the political turmoil of the 1950s. Fearing for his life, he fled to North America and was forced to take whatever job he could find.

▶ ▶ ▶ ▶▶▶▶▶

But Les was eager, and although a professional job eluded him, he soon had work on an airport construction crew. Then tragedy struck. He injured his leg at work. Les thought he had a big problem. He didn't know that he could have applied for some form of social assistance or compensation, so he immediately began looking for a job that he could do while his leg healed.

One day, as he was idly watching a window washer at work on an office building, he thought to himself, "I could do that. All I need are my arms to pull the rope and wash the windows." Sure enough, he impressed the owner of the cleaning company and before long he was straddling a tiny seat, attached to a long rope, cleaning windows.

"I couldn't believe how easy it was—and how much money it paid! I was sure I could do the job much more cheaply than the company I worked for, so I decided to bid on a contract of my own." A contract for a large office building came up and Les put in a cautious bid. "I didn't really want the contract, because I had no idea how I could do it, it was so big. But, I wanted to let them know I was in the business, so I bid what I thought was way too much for the job. To my amazement, I got it!"

Now Les had an even bigger problem—how to fill the contract. He solved it by hiring the company he had been working for to do it for him, and he took a commission off the top. He used the money to invest in new equipment. When he found the new equipment was inferior in design and construction, he used his engineering skills and started to redesign and repair the equipment, and that of other contractors.

By now his cleaning company was well established and he expanded his business to include cleaning parking lots. But the street-sweeping machines he used to clean parking lots were always breaking down. Les decided to design and build a better street-sweeper, and Riteway Manufacturing was born. His new machines sold well, but he had trouble keeping all his workers busy, so he looked for a new product. He found it in farm machinery, which eventually became his biggest line.

Les didn't stop there. When agriculture took a downturn, he focused on another problem his street-sweepers were encountering—potholes in the pavement. Les set out to design and build a new pothole-patching machine.

To Les Hulicsko, North America provided a wealth of opportunities to use his skills and ideas successfully.

Problems, Problems

But there's another way to look at this situation. You might say that for Les Hulicsko, North America was the land of problems. He couldn't get work as an engineer; he broke his leg; he couldn't fill his first cleaning contract; the machinery was inferior; he couldn't keep his workers fully occupied; and the potholes in the streets were hard on his sweepers. Nothing but trouble!

If that's what you thought, you'd be right. Les ran into a lot of problems. But, as you might have guessed by now, a problem can also be an opportunity! Look at it this way:

PROBLEM	*OPPORTUNITY*
Refugee	New homeland
Broken leg	Window cleaning
Contract too big	Subcontract and take commission
Inferior equipment	Design new equipment
Potholes	Pothole patcher

 Entrepreneurial opportunity is often disguised as a problem

If problems are everywhere—and few would argue with you about that—then opportunities are everywhere, too. Problems are an indication that something needs to be done or improved. A problem is a need, staring you in the face. Here are some examples:

PROBLEM	*NEED*
Car won't start	Better starter, battery, carburetor, maintenance
Shoes are uncomfortable	More choice in shoes, inserts for feet, foot-baths
Clothing wears out quickly	Better material, cheaper clothing, repair service
Weedy lawn	Weeding service, weed-free grass seed, chemicals
Family stress	Counseling service, family activities
Illiteracy	Better education, new books, better teaching techniques

A problem indicates a need and a need indicates an opportunity—because it points to a potential market. One of the best ways to spot opportunities is to listen to complainers.

Take a complainer to lunch, and pay attention

Some people complain and never do anything. Other people, called entrepreneurs, listen to complainers and try to solve the problems they howl about. See if you can list some potential opportunities that these common complaints might suggest. The first two are done for you:

COMPLAINT	*OPPORTUNITY*
"I hate winter."	Make winter more bearable for people
"My coffee's cold!"	Keep the coffee warm longer
"I can't talk to my kids."	_____
"I have too little time."	_____
"These buttons always fall off."	_____

▶ ▶ ▶ ▶▶▶▶

COMPLAINT	OPPORTUNITY
"This food is too expensive."	_____
"My tires seem to wear out so quickly."	_____
"I hate my hair."	_____
"Wool makes me itch."	_____
"I can't find a job."	_____

Take a look at your own personal problems, complaints, and needs and see if they reveal any opportunities.

EXERCISE 13

Task: To list problems and identify the needs they represent
Objective: To identify some opportunities

Use the following grid as a guide to explore both personal and community problems and needs. The categories and examples should help you focus:

PERSONAL PROBLEMS	NEEDS
Can't set new digital alarm clock	Customers need to be trained
_____	_____
_____	_____
_____	_____

COMMUNITY PROBLEMS	NEEDS
School bus funding cut	Transportation for school children
Bicycle theft on rise	Education/policing/innovative locks
_____	_____
_____	_____

Evaluation

Were you able to find needs related to every problem? If you have trouble doing these by yourself, get your family or friends to help. Remember, entrepreneurs use teams to help them achieve their goals. You'll be relieved to discover that two heads double the ideas and possibilities.

When you look at the needs you've listed, you're really looking at areas of potential opportunity. Each need points to a possible market that may be larger than just you. Later on, you'll learn how to find even more hidden opportunities and how to evaluate their potential.

Could you rephrase the question, please?

If you remember what problem solving was like in the classroom, you'll likely need to adjust your strategy. The problems you had to solve in school often had only one right answer. What is the capital of Italy? Rome. Period. How much is seven times eight? 56. No discussion. Of course, lots of teachers and schools aren't like that. Fortunately, more and more schools are inviting involvement from businesses in the form of work-experience education, or cooperative education, as it is sometimes called. These excellent programs allow students to learn and solve problems in an actual work environment.

But life isn't like most schools when it comes to problems and problem solving. Life doesn't serve up nice neat problems; it's full of messy problems—ones that have either no obvious solution or a whole raft of solutions that could all work.

Imagine you own a convenience store and you have a problem with teenagers who congregate in your parking lot and intimidate other customers. How do you solve this problem? You decide to ask each of five employees for their suggestions.

The first employee suggests that you call the police and have them order the teenagers to leave. The second suggests that you invite the teenagers in and talk to them so they will understand and leave. The third suggests putting up a sign informing people that the teenagers are harmless, and asking customers to come on in anyway. The fourth suggests moving the parking lot around to the back. The fifth suggests setting up the parking lot as an outdoor patio with a dance area, playing music the kids like, and selling refreshments to them outside.

All these suggestions have merit. They're all different because each employee sees a different problem. The first employee thinks it's a problem of enforcement; the second treats it as an educational challenge to teach the kids why they shouldn't congregate; the third employee wants to educate the other customers; the fourth says eliminate the reason for congregating in the first place and the fifth sees the problem as an opportunity to capitalize on your location's built-in popularity! Which problem do you want solved?

When you look at problems and try to determine what needs they reflect, remember that there may be many different kinds of needs that, if filled, would solve the problem. Later on you'll learn how to choose the best ones. But first, take a look at one more example of how problems can be opportunities in disguise.

PRO FILE

Entrepreneurs: Sonia and Gordon Jones
Enterprise: Peninsula Farm

"It all started with a cow named Daisy," says Sonia Jones, who, as a professor of Spanish, knew little about cows when she and her husband, Gordon, moved to the eastern seaboard where she was to begin her career.

When they bought a house in the country, a neighbor commented that the property would quickly become overgrown and suggested they'd need a cow to keep the grass under control. Enter Daisy, who indeed kept the grass neatly trimmed and, as a bonus, provided milk. But...

"I had no idea one cow could produce so much milk," Sonia recalls. "We couldn't possibly use it all. I moaned about my problem to a friend who had a health food store and she said, 'Why not make some of that fresh-milk yogurt you're famous for, since there's no fresh-milk yogurt on the market.' "

Sonia loved yogurt and knew how to make small batches, but she had no idea how to manufacture it in quantity. As a result, the Joneses threw out huge quantities of experimental yogurt, until they realized they could be feeding pigs with it instead. While the yogurt was being perfected, the fattened pigs were being turned into ham sandwiches, which were served to customers who were coming in growing numbers.

Soon the production process was bigger than the supply and the Joneses decided to start a full-sized dairy from scratch. Although they made mistakes regularly, they turned each one to their advantage. Rather than selling a machine that didn't dispense yogurt as advertised, they created yogurt cheese, a new product that it would dispense.

Today Peninsula Farm is still the smallest dairy in the area, but it enjoys the largest share of the yogurt market. And Sonia says, "When someone tells me, 'This is the best yogurt I've ever tasted,' or, 'This is the only yogurt I buy,' it's all worth it."

Problems are needs waiting to be filled. Although needs and wants aren't always the same thing, wants are also harbingers of opportunity. For example, we all have a need for food, but we may want less-fattening food. A want is usually a more specific need.

Opportunities and ideas: siblings, but not twins

By now you may be wondering if great ideas are even part of the process of entrepreneurship. "Don't people get rich by coming up with great ideas?" you may ask. Actually, no, they don't usually do it that way. Entrepreneurs have learned that it's far more important to identify an opportunity first, and then come up with an idea that will best exploit it. Opportunities and ideas are closely related, but for our purposes they're not the same thing.

The world may or may not beat a path to your door

The main difference between an idea and an opportunity is that an opportunity points to a potential market and an idea is a specific response to that proven need. For example, if you live in a community overrun by mice, that problem points to an opportunity: the need to reduce the mouse population. A better mousetrap is a likely idea. However, if you simply dream up a better mousetrap, with no thought about where mouse problems exist or how severe they are, you will have to go looking for your market. And, as the saying goes, "nothing is lonelier than an idea in search of a market."

Look at it this way: You may have an idea, such as a new form of dentures made out of rock candy but it may not represent an opportunity. While opportunities are common, ideas are a dime a dozen.

That's why Chapter 4 is devoted to the process of generating entrepreneurial ideas. And that's why you need to understand the role and nature of opportunity first.

Here's a definition that will help:

Opportunity: A need, want, problem, or challenge that can be addressed through an innovative entrepreneurial idea.

The Challenge of Change

Television threatens radio. Videos are the end of the drive-in movie. A robot welder replaces 10 human welders. Cheaper imported toasters wipe out local toaster businesses. Computers replace typewriters and cash registers. Environmental concerns slow forestry production. The thinning ozone layer causes beach businesses to close. Borders between countries disappear and so do import-export rules. The population grows more aged, straining health and financial resources.

We live in a world of unprecedented massive social, political, and technological change. As a result, we also live in a world of unprecedented problems.

You're an entrepreneur in search of opportunity—of problems that need to be solved and challenges to be met! You welcome massive change and all it brings because you know that great opportunities ride its crest and you know where to look for them.

⟨ KEY POINT ⟩ **Entrepreneurs lead, welcome, and thrive on change**

Technological change cuts through society like a double-edged sword, sometimes creating more problems than it solves. But it always creates plenty of opportunities along the way. Tools, appliances, manufacturing, and entertainment devices are becoming smaller, more powerful, more complex, and more intelligent. One of the products of entrepreneurship is better-quality products. For example, look what happened to recorded music technology.

Remember phonograph records? Depending on your age, you may recall those little black plastic discs you'd spin on your hi-fi. The more you played them, the more they hissed and popped. They weren't perfect, but they were all there was—until plastic recording tape came along in 1950.

Actually, recording tape had been invented in 1898, but came into use in recording studios only at the end of the 1940s. The tape-recording machines were large and heavy. So, music was recorded on tape and then transferred to vinyl records. Most people didn't own a tape recorder since they weren't portable and tapes of popular tunes were largely nonexistent—until the transistor changed everything.

Invented in 1948, the transistor shrank the size of a radio to that of a package of cigarettes by 1955. If it could shrink radios, then what about tape recorders? Entrepreneurs were at work. By 1964 the reels of tape were shrunk and packaged into neat little eight-track cassettes, which soon shrank to even smaller and more popular four-track cassettes, so the tape wouldn't have to be touched by hand. Musical entrepreneurs realized they could sell music on these tapes, just like records. The little tapes became so popular they began to rival the sale of records, which survived until the compact disc (CD) appeared in 1983.

It was 10 short years from the introduction of the transistor radio to the cassette, and 20 years more to the CD and digital audio tape (DAT). Much industry carnage happened in those 30 or so years. But today we can carry a machine the size of a small pocket novel, and, wearing a headset that's almost weightless, we can walk on the beach enjoying a recording of an orchestra that's of such high quality, it is rivalled only by the original live concert.

Technological carnage, entrepreneurial heaven

When the tidal wave of technological change swept through the home entertainment industry, those who weren't prepared were washed away to sea: vinyl wholesalers; record-pressing companies; and people who sold and manufactured needles, record-players, album covers, vacuum tubes, and even shelving for albums. Reel-to-reel tape recorders disappeared and so will audiotape cassettes. But those entrepreneurs who were prepared for change didn't moan the passing of old equipment and techniques. Instead, they flourished by manufacturing, selling, and maintaining all the new products the technology made possible.

EXERCISE 14

Task: To list recent changes in technology and what they threaten
Objective: To identify possible opportunities disguised as technological change

Look around at your immediate environment. Can you see evidence of technological change? Do you see one product, like an audiotape cassette, at the end of its life and another, like a CD, in its prime? In this exercise you can practice examining the effects of technological change. On the left is a list of well-known everyday products. You can add to this list, if you want. In the three columns on the right, fill in the blanks to list the needs or wants the products address, the technological advancement that made them possible, and the product they replace or threaten. The first two are done for you, and random clues are provided throughout the exercise.

PRODUCT/ SERVICE	NEED/ WANT	TECHNOLOGY	REPLACES/ THREATENS
automobile	transportation	engine/roads	horse, train, walking
home freezer	food preservative	electricity	icebox, ice supplier
television			
VCR		miniaturization	
cable TV			
personal computer			
answering machine	communication		
voice mail		digital recording	
Teflon pan		Teflon	
satellite dish			
heart transplant		special drugs	

Evaluation

If you often found more than one possibility for each blank, you're learning this important lesson well. In this case you will have learned that technology makes new products and services possible and, at the same time, renders old ones obsolete. Sometimes technology that's created to solve one problem ends up solving others that weren't even considered in the first place. You may recall the famous glue that wasn't sticky enough that resulted in the invention of sticky notes. When you choose your venture, avoid hitching your star to something based on technology that is on its way out, unless there are other problems or needs it could satisfy. Pop cases are obsolete in many places, but they make great storage bins and shelving blocks.

EXERCISE 15

Task: To make myself aware of technological advances as they happen
Objective: To identify possible opportunities and pitfalls

This is an ongoing exercise that, once started, you'll likely do for the rest of your life. It's never too late to start, but the sooner you sharpen your sensitivity, the better. New technologies spring up everywhere, but they tend to be concentrated in a few key areas: communication/entertainment, transportation, manufacturing, and health. They also tend to spill over into each other's arenas. By keeping abreast of as many new developments as possible, you might uncover an opportunity to put someone else's technology to work for you in a new way. But first, you have to know about it.

Start by scanning journals and newspapers for stories on technological breakthroughs. See if you can find magazines or journals that feature or include as many of the technologies listed on the left as possible. Write down the names of the publications and then, when you scan them, note anything new in the column on the right.

TECHNOLOGY	PUBLICATION	WORTH NOTING
Communication		
computers	Inside Computers	10 GB hard-drive
television		
fax machines		
telephones		
printers		
cameras/film		
photocopying		
Transportation		
cars/trucks	Carworld	Non-corroding body panels
motorcycles		
ships/boats		
air/spacecraft		
trains		
bicycles		

Technology	Publication	Worth Noting
Manufacturing/processing		
cars	Shop News	Robotic welders
electronics		
housing		
steel/metal		
wood/paper		
food		
Health/nutrition		
medical	Local newspaper	Healing through hypnosis
natural foods		
exercise		
weight loss		

Evaluation

No doubt you discovered some amazing new developments in your browsing. Of course, you won't likely be interested in every type of technology listed above, but if you make a habit of noting discoveries of all types when you see them, and those in your areas of interest in particular, you'll have a pretty good idea of what changes are coming and what they'll mean to existing technologies. Add oddball publications to your bedtime and vacation reading, and make a habit of talking to and questioning people who announce, "Boy, wait till you see what they're coming out with now!"

 Entrepreneurs keep abreast of new technology

Social change

Technology can change society. For example, telephone calls replace visits, reducing physical human contact. Two decades ago movie going was a family and social event. When friends and neighbors went to the movies, their experience went beyond merely passively viewing a movie. It included social intercourse, fun, and courtship. The VCR has fundamentally changed our social values about movie going.

Meanwhile, many cinema owners decided to co-opt the new technology and simply added video sales and rental services in their lobbies.

Other forces change society as well as technology, such as education and immigration. Cultures, races, and religions merge, change, and reform. In the process, values also change and create new and challenging needs.

If you're an immigrant, you likely have a long list of problems you encountered as you tried to adapt to a new country. Those problems might be a good place for you to start looking for opportunities. Problems you've experienced personally are usually the best ones to start with.

Society is constantly changing, rendering old problems and solutions obsolete and creating new ones.

Here, for example, are some changes that are common in many countries:

- Students are staying in school longer and are developing habits of lifelong learning. Possible needs: More and better schools, courses of study, teacher training, apprenticeship programs.

- People are waiting longer to get married and, when they do, they're having fewer children. Possible needs: Adult recreation; upscale children's clothing.

- Systems of government are changing from state-controlled to market-driven. Possible needs: Business and entrepreneurship training; consumer education.

- Men and women are more health-conscious, exercise more, and choose foods on the basis of nutrition as much as taste. Possible needs: Health and exercise clubs, specialty food restaurants, fitness clothing and accessories.

- Traditional roles of the sexes are changing. Men and women are waiting longer to get married, and are both pursuing active careers while they delay having children. Possible needs: Ask Marsali MacIver.

PRO FILE

Entrepreneur: Marsali MacIver

Enterprise: Neat Freaks

Even while she was working in sales for a major publication, Marsali MacIver was looking for a venture she could call her own. She prepared herself by studying the changes happening in society around her; she was looking for opportunity—looking for needs and problems. She didn't overlook her own experience, either.

"I'm a 'neat freak,' " says Marsali. "I like a neat, clean place to live, but I never seemed to have enough time to clean my apartment. I figured I wasn't the only one with that problem." Marsali listened and what she heard were other people who said the same thing: they don't have time to clean. Times had changed. With most members of households pursuing active careers, no one was left to do the daily housekeeping, and the traditional cleaning services didn't match their new lifestyles. They weren't interested in sharing their lives with a maid or a housekeeper; they just wanted their residences cleaned—and quickly.

Marsali took the cue. She quit her job and started Neat Freaks. Neat Freaks was to be no ordinary cleaning service. What a traditional cleaner would do in a day, Neat Freaks, working in teams of three and four workers, does in one hour. In and out. When the client returns home, the kitchen and bathroom are spotless and even the picture frames have been dusted.

As president of the company, Marsali didn't do the cleaning herself. She kept busy hiring crews and finding new customers. After 10 years of successful entrepreneurship, Marsali sold the company at a profit and looked for new challenges. Today, she is teaching marketing as part of an entrepreneurship program at a local college. In addition, she's running for office as a city councillor and continues to scan the horizon for new opportunities.

Entrepreneurs see new needs in social changes

Look around you and ask yourself, what problems or needs are being created by the changes in society? For example, the growth of feminism is having a tremendous impact on society. More women are entering the workforce and leaving homemaking to men and to hired help. Women are changing the traditionally male workplace and the way business is done.

Women now hold jobs that were traditionally dominated by men. What challenges are created when women get involved in professional hockey and football, heavy construction, building maintenance, politics, and corporate leadership? And what challenges do these changes present to men, to teachers, and to the media who report these changes?

Society is constantly changing and with each change, opportunities are created. For example, until 1955, popular music was played for and by adults. Then along came rock'n'roll, which fundamentally changed popular music as well as the relationship between adults and the teenagers. Entrepreneurs with an eye for opportunity recognized that rock'n'roll wasn't just a new musical fad; it was a social revolution, and a huge new market had just been created. Today, young people consume the lion's share of the multi-billion-dollar music industry and those who saw change coming and were ready for it made fortunes.

Try a new hobby...spotting trends

When you walk down the street, try looking at what's going on around you. If you're like most people, you tend to think of the street and its social activity as being random and reactive. But the more you watch people, the more you realize that their behavior is far more predictable than not. Humans follow patterns of behavior—avoiding certain parts of the street, travelling at specific times, purchasing similar things, and using them in similar ways. By sensitizing yourself to recognize patterns in tastes and styles, you'll be able to spot changes in those patterns when they happen.

Here are some clues to look for.

- Changes in fashion trends: more or fewer men wearing shorts; army fatigues that quickly follow military activity; more or less short hair, long hair, curly, and straight hair; shorter or longer skirts; floral ties, striped ties or no ties; more or fewer running shoes, sandals, bare feet, and army boots

- Changes in transportation: more or fewer bikes, motorcycles, cars, and limousines; more or fewer walkers and runners; more or fewer diesel buses, electric trolleys, freeways, and moving sidewalks; more or less public transit

- Changes in eating habits: more or fewer fast-food outlets, sidewalk cafés, and exotic eateries; more or less health food and low-fat food; more or fewer grocery stores; more or less imported food

- Changes in ways of doing business: shorter or longer meetings; fewer meetings and more phone calls; more or fewer faxes and more or less use of computers and modems; more or less formal business attire; deals taking less or more time; more or less cosmopolitan business practices and etiquette; cheaper or more expensive lunches, hotel rooms, and conference sites; more or less time for family and personal life

- Changes in teen trends: fashions, styles, slang, hangouts, pastimes (computer games, arcades, dancing, rollerblading, skateboarding, card-trading, mini-business startups), and attitudes (more or less respectful, attentive, interested, bored, independent).

When you notice changes and trends, research them to find out how widespread they are. You might possibly create a venture to catch the market before other competitors get the jump on you.

Newspapers are a great way to track changes in society. The headlines alone should get your entrepreneurial antennae quivering:

TRADE PACT SIGNED

CRIME ON THE RISE

SPORTS SHOW SOLD OUT

SENIOR CITIZENS' HOME OVERLOADED

IMMIGRATION UP

Where others see random behavior, entrepreneurs see patterns

Is the crime rate really rising? That would mean there's a growing need for people to feel more secure, which might create opportunities in: security systems, bodyguard and protection services, burglarproof windows, counseling services for criminals, crime prevention programs for communities, and insurance sales. If the overloaded seniors' home is really a sign of an aging population, what kinds of needs might result?

Now it's your turn.

EXERCISE 16

Task: To list some possible needs resulting from social changes
Objective: To improve my ability to recognize opportunities

Assume some of the headlines at the bottom of page 78 indicate trends. For each trend below, list some needs it might create. The categories will help focus your thoughts, and the first suggestions are designed to get you started.

Trend:
An aging population

Needs created:

FOOD/HEALTH	SHELTER	FAMILY/SOCIAL	FINANCIAL
palliative care	homes for aged	entertainment	investment programs

Trend:
Increasing interest in spectator sports

Needs created:

HUMAN RESOURCES	SITE OR LOCATION	MEDIA BROADCAST	EDUCATION
players	arenas	packaged programs	athletic training

► ► ► ►►►►►

Trend:
Increasing immigration

Needs created:

FOOD/HEALTH	EMPLOYMENT	FAMILY/SOCIAL	EDUCATION
specialty foods	counseling	community centers	language training

Trend:
Your choice:
Needs created:

Evaluation

Are you finding it easier to relate opportunity to problems and challenges? Are you starting to look at newspapers in a new way? Do you listen more closely to the complaints of your friends and co-workers? If so, you're developing the observational skills of an entrepreneur.

Through the Window of Opportunity

You may have heard the phrase "window of opportunity" and wondered what it means. It's simply a metaphor that represents the likelihood of entrepreneurial success, depending on how wide the window is open, how long it will remain open, and who can fit through the opening.

These variables reflect the dynamic nature of entrepreneurship. Just as society and technology are constantly changing, so the opportunities they present are constantly appearing and disappearing. And just as those opportunities are more appropriate to some entrepreneurs with specific skills and interests, they are less appropriate to others.

By now you'll agree that it's not hard to identify opportunities. In fact, you may have already discovered more than you could ever possibly pursue. It's time to narrow the possibilities to those that are best for you. Let's look at one example and use the window metaphor to evaluate its potential for success.

You've listened to your friends, co-workers, and people on the street. Newspapers reinforce your growing belief that there's a significant demand for children's designer clothing. Could there be a window of opportunity for you?

How big is the window?

1. How large is the market for these products?
2. How many people can afford them?
3. Who are these buyers? (Parents? Grandparents?) How old are the buyers? (Young parents? Older parents?)
4. Is this a local or widespread phenomenon? (Does it span communities? States or provinces? Countries?)
5. How old are the children who wear these clothes? (One to three years? Three to ten years?)

Is the window opening or closing?

1. Is the market growing or shrinking? What is the current birth rate?
2. Are there lots of new shops and products already in evidence? Are any businesses closing? Why?
3. Is your economy in a recession, growing rapidly or recovering slowly?

How wide is the window open for you?

1. Do you already have experience in this area? Related experience?
2. How much do you know about fashion, design, children, parents, retailing, wholesaling, and manufacturing?
3. Is there a small (or niche) market that is being overlooked by everyone else?
4. How motivated are you to go after this opportunity? (Lifelong dream? Never thought of it before now? Try it for awhile, then move on?)
5. Can you build a team that complements your skills?
6. Can you raise the necessary money to get started?

Conclusion

You have identified a large, clear window of opportunity that is wide open for you, if the following are true:

• The trend is growing.
• The market is large and relatively unserviced.
• Existing businesses are thriving and expanding.
• The economy is healthy.

- You have lots of related experience.
- You have innovative ideas on how to improve products or service.
- You are highly motivated.
- You can assemble a talented team.
- And you can get the money to start up.

But, if any of those variables don't reflect your research or personal situation, the window may be closed to you, while it remains open to others. If you know something nobody else does, the window may be opening for you and closing for them.

On the other hand, the window of retailing may be closed to you but, because you may have accessed an innovative manufacturing, design, or distribution process, you may have a large, wide open window of your very own. Similarly, you may have discovered that retailers have not bothered servicing a large, isolated, or international market that you're able to exploit. As this window opens for you, it may close for them.

 Entrepreneurs strive to know why an opportunity exists for them

Niche markets

When big windows of opportunity open, they tend to stay open for a long time. For example, automobiles and consumer electronics flew through enormous windows that are opening still wider even today. But the entrepreneurs who fly through those windows are as large as their products and markets. How can a budding entrepreneur get into the game?

For many entrepreneurs, the answer lies in niche or specialty markets. Large manufacturers and distributors often can't afford to service the top and bottom of their markets. They deal in volume and are able to compete because of economies of scale (it's cheaper, per item, to make lots of something than just one or two items). Look at the clothing in your local department store. You'll find lots of choice in the middle price range and in the most common sizes. You won't find really large or small sizes or very cheap or expensive items.

That might mean there are large, small, rich, or poor customers in your community who aren't being serviced. It's possible that you could open a large-size clothing shop or a business that sells nothing over $10. If you're the only business like that in town, you've opened a small window of opportunity very wide.

Some opportunities stare everybody in the face but, because they're considered unattractive occupations, most people turn away and close the window. You might not be averse to doing jobs other people can't stand, such as:

• developing new ways to sort garbage into categories for recycling
• introducing innovative toilets and septic and sewer systems
• finding new ways to dispose of toxic waste.

Do you know a thing or two about waste and garbage? You may have expert knowledge and skills that could turn problems into success!

Some other challenges that people tend to shy away from include: caring for people with special health needs; treating alcohol, tobacco, and other forms of drug addiction; treating gambling addictions; counseling terminally ill people; offering funeral and mortuary services; pet and pest control; and work involving physical labor. If you have experience or interest in any of these areas, don't overlook possible opportunities there.

There are books that discuss niche markets, or gaps, as they're sometimes called. Ask your local librarian about them if you're interested in exploring such opportunities.

 Entrepreneurs tune in to the obvious

Recycling product ideas

Have you ever heard a tune on the radio or television that has a new sound, but you remember it as an old song? It happens all the time. Current pop stars often get new hits by re-recording old songs. The window of opportunity opens and closes over time for all kinds of products, services, and ventures.

No one would argue that the car replaced the horse and buggy, but for some entrepreneurs the horse and buggy has found a new use—transporting tourists on scenic tours, for example. And horses are still used for pony rides, rodeos, horse-racing, and some farm work. Old products can be rediscovered and used in an entirely new set of circumstances.

Earlier in the chapter you read about Peninsula Farm and how Sonia and Gordon Jones created a new product in an old industry. Lee Crowley, on the other hand, found opportunity by using an old product in an old way.

Entrepreneur: Lee Crowley

Enterprise: Avalon Dairy

Lee Crowley was born into the dairy business. After flirting with other lines of work, Lee came home to take over Avalon Dairy, which had been in the family for almost 100 years. Lee modernized some of the dairy's operations, but he didn't mess with the container that had carried Avalon milk for decades—the glass milk bottle.

The milk bottle had long since lost favor with other dairies who had replaced it with the familiar cardboard container in the 1960s. Avalon decided to keep the bottle, and its customers were glad they did. There's something special about the tinkling of milk bottles when the delivery person arrives at your door. And people claim milk tastes better out of a bottle, too. When he's asked if that's true, Lee says, "All I know is this. Cook a nice meal and eat it from a paper plate and then try the same meal on a china plate. Which tastes better? People choose the china every time."

The milk bottle helped Avalon keep a niche market of loyal customers, but then society changed. Suddenly, the cardboard container became part of a growing waste problem. In Lee's community, garbage had to be stored and then transported by truck and barge long distances at significant costs. The biggest culprit was paper and cardboard waste. Meanwhile, the glass bottle could be refilled many times before it was simply recycled into more glass bottles. The glass bottle is also completely nontoxic. When a study appeared, showing that there might be residual toxins in cardboard milk containers, Lee's market grew by 100 %, almost overnight.

"And that's big enough," says Lee. "I don't want to get too big. But, I do believe the milk bottle is an important part of preserving our environment. There's more to business than just making money."

Opportunities and change...a review

Like a farmer's plow, change cuts through society burying old, established ways of doing things, and leaving in its wake fresh fertile soil, ready for the new seeds of entrepreneurship to take root. Old technology is buried as it becomes the medium of growth for new technology. Old social values change and turn over, rendering the structures they supported obsolete, while new values and structures emerge.

As an entrepreneur, you needn't fear change; you should encourage it, lead it, and make it the medium of your enterprise. Where others shrink from change, you should actively pursue it as a partner. The changes that are sweeping and the most frightening bring the most opportunity for innovative solutions. Remember, you are an entrepreneur, not an opportunist. Rather than profiting from the misery of others, you seek innovative solutions to new and persistent problems. Your purpose is to make life better, not worse.

Here are some of the most common and obvious challenges of change:

Political and social change

- Communist countries move toward market economies
- Traditional male/female roles undergo massive change
- Massive national debts turn political agendas upside down
- Religious wars and conflicts escalate

- Nuclear weapons proliferate
- Terrorism continues unabated
- Voters in democracies grow increasingly cynical about politicians
- Refugees and immigrants choke existing social services
- Racial and linguistic intolerance threatens social harmony
- Millions of people starve to death annually
- Millions of homeless children populate urban centres
- AIDS and other diseases reach worldwide epidemic proportions.

New communications and entertainment technology

- Wars are widely broadcast and seem like TV entertainment programs
- Hundreds of TV channels become available to consumers
- Cellular telephones access people in cars and in remote locations
- Children become addicted to video games
- Computers replace typewriters and postal services.

New military technology

- Smart bombs can select highly specific targets
- Spy satellites can photograph license plate numbers on earth
- Aircraft can be made invisible to radar
- Handheld devices can pinpoint location anywhere on earth.

New medical and genetic technology

- Gender of fetuses can be determined in the womb
- Plants and animals can be cloned
- Genetic engineering can correct flaws of nature
- Cosmetic surgery can alter physical appearance
- Death can be delayed hours and weeks
- Severed limbs can be reattached
- Animal organs can be transplanted into humans.

New computer technology

- People around the globe can communicate through networks
- Every citizen is recorded in a database
- People can publish books at home
- Complex mathematical calculations take seconds instead of hours
- Cash is being replaced by plastic cards with magnetic strips
- Cumulative knowledge is growing at a tremendous rate.

New food technology

- Chemicals are removed from food
- Hypoallergenic foods are being produced
- Natural flavors are chemically synthesized
- Organic food production shows rapid growth
- Synthetic and calorie-free fat is being produced
- Delicate foods are preserved for global distribution.

Economic change and globalization of marketplace

- Foreign products compete with local products
- Manufacturers move to countries where production is cheap
- Inefficient production processes become obsolete
- Product quality improves while prices become cheaper
- Traditional jobs and skills become obsolete
- Workers face layoffs and retraining
- Domestic businesspeople learn international trading skills
- New international trading agreements are forged.

You may feel tiny and insignificant when you're faced with such enormous changes and problems. But by identifying even a small problem or challenge that you can pursue as an entrepreneurial opportunity, you are playing the most important of all roles in society—you are showing others how to deal with change and how to solve problems. You become an employer and an instrument of economic growth and, most important of all, you create a meaningful and satisfying life for yourself.

 Entrepreneurs solve problems and create new opportunities

Home is where the opportunities are, too

You were promised at the beginning of this chapter that you'd soon have too many opportunities. You may now believe that you live in the Golden Age of Opportunity, but amidst all these possible opportunities, you may wonder where to start. If you feel that all the sources of opportunity listed in this chapter are too daunting for you, take heart. Most entrepreneurs get started by finding opportunities right on their doorsteps or, more commonly, on their employers' doorsteps.

If you're an employee, start looking for opportunities at work. Maybe you can find a way to improve your company's competitiveness and create an opportunity for yourself at the same time. Here's one entrepreneur who did just that.

PRO FILE

Entrepreneur: Grant Jack

Enterprise: Grant's Woodworking

Grant Jack is a skilled tradesperson who likes his job at the local auto parts manufacturing firm. Like other workers, he worries about the ups and downs of the industry and about looming layoffs. But unlike most of his co-workers, Grant is also an entrepreneur. In his spare time he builds and sells lawn furniture and, with his wife, Lisa, he breeds and sells purebred dogs.

Grant has developed a nose for opportunity and an eye for better ways of doing things. While unpacking crates at work one day, he thought about the Styrofoam packaging that was being used once and then thrown away. "This looks pretty wasteful. I wonder if I could make these items out of wood?" he thought. He approached his boss and asked how much the company was paying for their existing materials. As a skilled carpenter, he knows what wood costs and how long it takes to make things, so he did some quick calculations and said, "I'll make them for you for half that price, and you can reuse them over and over again." His employer

jumped at the offer and soon Grant had all the extra work he could handle.

He didn't stop there, though. Grant noticed that his company bought new plastic waste buckets for $6 each, paid extra for lids that weren't always used, and then used the buckets just once and threw them away. He also noticed similar buckets out behind the local fast-food chicken outlet; they had been used for cooking oil and thrown away. The fast-food franchise quickly took him up on his offer to purchase all their buckets at $1 each. After a quick cleaning, he sold them to his company for $2 each with lids extra.

Grant Jack isn't ready to quit his job just yet, but as an entrepreneurial employee, he's not likely to be laid off, either. Meanwhile, the extra income has paid for the first vacation he and his wife have ever had, and also for his new chicken-and-egg operation. He sells eggs to friends, neighbors, and co-workers, and when the laying stops, he sells the chickens and starts over.

Have you noticed inefficiencies in the company where you're employed? Could you improve the production process or the product itself? What about supplying lunch or cleaning services? Listen to your co-workers when they complain about how things are done, or which products work and which ones don't. Maybe there's an opportunity for you to start a small venture on the side.

You don't have to become a full-time entrepreneur overnight. In fact, most entrepreneurs keep their day jobs for as long as possible. They use their wages or salaries to finance their ventures and keep the job as a fall-back position should the venture run into trouble. If this is what you plan to do, don't think of yourself as any less of an entrepreneur; think of yourself as a smart and realistic entrepreneur. Remember, you have to learn to walk before you can run.

Your workplace as a source of niche market opportunities

Earlier in the chapter you learned that large companies usually concentrate on the largest markets, often leaving smaller markets untapped. You might be in a position to learn all you need to know about manufacturing a product or servicing a particular clientele and, by giving your skills a little twist, you might be able to direct your efforts to a small unserviced market.

For example, if you work in a hotel, you'd know most of what you need to start a bed-and-breakfast business. If you're in sales, you could start your own line of specialty products—but don't step on your employer in the process. Sometimes you can pick up your employer's leavings.

PRO FILE

Entrepreneur: Gilles Bourque
Enterprise: BoNeon

Gilles Bourque hadn't planned on becoming an entrepreneur. He was quite happy working for his employer as a sign maker, especially after he was put in charge of the new production line of neon signs. Gilles discovered that he loved working with neon and after a couple of years, he became quite skilled at the process, which is not easy to learn.

But his employer didn't share Gilles' enthusiasm for the relatively small neon sign market, and when it was dropped from the product line, Gilles decided to pick it up himself and start his own full-time neon sign business.

Today, Gilles' main product is neon signs, but, to protect his downside, he has evolved some new products for other niche markets so he can keep his enterprise healthy and independent.

How about you?

When your employer drops a line of products, do you find out why? You should. In fact, your employer might even help you pick up an abandoned line, just to keep customers happy.

EXERCISE 17

Task: To review my potential opportunities
Objective: To choose the best entrepreneurial opportunity for me

By now you're likely eager to get started on your venture. But first, you have to make sure you've picked the right opportunity. In this exercise you'll narrow down your possibilities to one or two and then do a thorough evaluation of them to determine your window of opportunity.

Select three opportunities you think suit you best, going back over this chapter for help if needed. Don't choose only on the basis of how much money you think they'll make for you. Remember, you haven't yet determined the precise entrepreneurial idea you'll pursue. You're just looking for the area of opportunity. For example, let's say you've decided on the general area: food service. Later you'll decide whether you'll start a restaurant, grocery wholesale or whatever, then what kind of restaurant, and so on.

Use the following schedule of priorities and rate each item on a scale of one to five.

Opportunity 1: _____

Is the need, want, problem, challenge:

	No				Yes
Proven to be real?	1	2	3	4	5
Widespread?	1	2	3	4	5
Important to others?	1	2	3	4	5
Under-serviced?	1	2	3	4	5
Improperly serviced?	1	2	3	4	5
Clearly defined?	1	2	3	4	5
Within my area of expertise?	1	2	3	4	5
Thoroughly researched?	1	2	3	4	5
The best one I can find?	1	2	3	4	5
Something I will enjoy pursuing?	1	2	3	4	5

Total score: _____

Opportunity 2: _____

Is the need, want, problem, challenge:

	No				Yes
Proven to be real?	1	2	3	4	5
Widespread?	1	2	3	4	5
Important to others?	1	2	3	4	5
Under-serviced?	1	2	3	4	5
Improperly serviced?	1	2	3	4	5
Clearly defined?	1	2	3	4	5
Within my area of expertise?	1	2	3	4	5
Thoroughly researched?	1	2	3	4	5
The best one I can find?	1	2	3	4	5
Something I will enjoy pursuing?	1	2	3	4	5

Total score: _____

▶ ▶ ▶ ▶▶▶▶▶

Opportunity 3: _____

Is the need, want, problem, challenge:

	No				Yes
Proven to be real?	1	2	3	4	5
Widespread?	1	2	3	4	5
Important to others?	1	2	3	4	5
Under-serviced?	1	2	3	4	5
Improperly serviced?	1	2	3	4	5
Clearly defined?	1	2	3	4	5
Within my area of expertise?	1	2	3	4	5
Thoroughly researched?	1	2	3	4	5
The best one I can find?	1	2	3	4	5
Something I will enjoy pursuing?	1	2	3	4	5

Total score: _____

Evaluation

The opportunity with the highest total will likely be the best one for you. But, there are other variables to consider. For example, if the opportunity hasn't been proven to be real—that is, you may think it's an opportunity, but you're just guessing—it's likely most of the other points won't tell you much. You must do research, or have research done for you. Survey people and study the market, the problems, and other ventures that have tried but failed, or tried and been successful.

If the opportunity is not within your area of expertise, how close is it? If you know how to sell cars, you shouldn't have much trouble learning how to sell children's clothing, for example. But, if your experience includes only bookkeeping, you may not be wise to try the restaurant business. However, all this notwithstanding, anybody, including you, can learn new things, if you're motivated enough.

Now that you've identified your best opportunity, hold that thought

First, you'll need a bit of practice. You don't want to use your very best opportunity for practice purposes any more than you'd want to learn to drive at Le Mans. Your very best opportunity deserves your very best shot, and you won't be able to deliver that until you've had a run or two at some small problem-solving exercises.

EXERCISE 18

Task: To identify a simple, short-term challenge or problem
Objective: To practice small-scale problem solving

Entrepreneurship turns on identifying, clarifying, and solving problems. In this exercise you'll identify a good practical problem that needs an entrepreneurial solution. You're going to be using this little venture in the next chapter, so have it ready.

Start by looking at some relatively small problems or challenges around your home.

Maybe:
- your relatives and friends complain that you don't stay in touch
- your family seems to eat out too much
- you are physically unfit
- your family doesn't spend enough time together.

Get the picture? Let's say your problem is that you're physically unfit and unhappy about it. How can this problem be an opportunity in disguise?

Perhaps, in order to get fit, you might:
- join a health club and meet new people
- try running and develop a new appreciation for nature
- take up exercising and strengthen your willpower along with your body
- learn how to cook more nutritious meals
- walk more, and use the time to think and reflect
- take up and learn a team sport
- buy and learn a great deal about athletic equipment.

The last seven suggestions are more in the nature of entrepreneurial ideas.

My challenge or problem is: _____

_____

In the next chapter you'll learn how to pick and evaluate the best ideas, starting with one that is the result of the above exercise. But first, here's a summary of the key points from Chapter 3.

 Summary

Entrepreneurial opportunity is often disguised as a problem
Entrepreneurs lead, welcome, and thrive on change
Entrepreneurs keep abreast of new technology
Entrepreneurs see new needs in social changes
Where others see random behavior, entrepreneurs see patterns
Entrepreneurs strive to know why an opportunity exists for them
Entrepreneurs tune in to the obvious
Entrepreneurs solve problems and create new opportunities

4 Ideas and Innovation

*"Aye, laddie,
I've spent most of my
life thinking up crazy
ways of doing things."*
🐿 SCOTTY, CHIEF ENGINEER,
THE STARSHIP *ENTERPRISE*

By now you should know that there are no great ideas without great opportunities. Opportunities are problems and challenges for which ideas are the solutions. For example, in the practice lesson at the end of the last chapter you came up with a small problem (opportunity), such as the need to become more physically fit. You know that there are a number of possible ways (ideas) to become more fit. This chapter will show you how to:

• brainstorm as many ideas as possible
• choose the best ones
• evaluate them carefully
• recognize and practice innovation
• understand and manage resistance to change.

If you think you have to invent a new idea, you'll learn that inventing is for inventors. You are an innovator, and there's a world of difference between the two. If you think that ideas are rare, you'll learn that they're really a dime a dozen. And if that makes you wonder why there aren't more tycoons, it's because most people haven't learned how to apply the whole process of entrepreneurship to venture creation. Ideas often sound great, but unless they're examined, tested, and put into the hands of competent entrepreneurs, they're just beer talk. You'll learn that it's a lot easier to think up ideas than it is to make them work. Creating ideas requires creativity—no surprise, there—but the good part is that you can learn to become more creative.

Is Creativity Innate?

How creative are you? Are you always thinking up new and crazy ways of doing things or do you leave the creative stuff to others? Do you ever wonder how those people get so creative? Are they born that way?

Working backwards for a moment, consider: if creativity is an innate characteristic, why are there so many creativity workshops, seminars, courses, and experts ready to teach it? Some people think that creativity can't be learned and can't be taught, so why bother? I believe that creative people get that way by practicing. They learn techniques to enhance creativity and then they improve them. You can become more creative, too. It's an open-ended activity, and one you can always get better at.

Join the dots

Try joining all nine dots below by drawing four connected straight lines without lifting your pencil off the page.

• • •

• • •

• • •

Yes, there is a trick, of sorts. And there is probably more than one way to complete the puzzle. Before you turn the page for the answer, here's a clue: Don't impose unnecessary restrictions on yourself.

If you weren't able to solve the puzzle, you might have been blocking your creativity with unnecessary assumptions:

• Did you assume that the dots framed a rectangle?

• Did you assume that you couldn't go beyond the corners and white space?

We often assume restrictive rules that may or may not be relevant to the problem we're trying to solve. Being creative often means breaking rules.

What it isn't

To understand better what creativity is, let's look at what it isn't. It isn't logical, for starters. Creating ideas is a right-brain activity. Right brain refers to the artistic or creative hemisphere of the brain; the left hemisphere is said to govern logical or rational thinking. You won't come up with particularly creative ideas by tracing their logical progression from proven premises. To be creative you have to break rules, practice non sequiturs, and set your mind free to soar at random.

Humans are creatures of habit. Theater patrons tend to return to the same seats each time they return to the same theater; commuters take the same route to work, regardless of other possible, more interesting, ways to get there; we eat the same kinds of food at the same times of the day. Try this. Cross your arms. Comfy? Now, cross them the other way. Not comfy, right? Did you know you always crossed your arms the same way? You're likely doing all kinds of other things the same way, too.

If you're in a rut, it's hard to see beyond it.

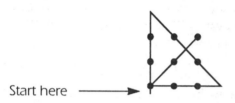

Start here

Creativity 101

Break your routine; climb out of those ruts! If you find the following childish (and yes, children do love these kinds of activities), keep in mind that you're trying to be childlike, playful, and a bit silly. It's really just a matter of seeing the world, however playfully, from another perspective. Try, if you dare:

- eating breakfast in the evening
- striking up conversations with people at bus stops
- removing all the chairs in the boardroom before a meeting
- eating without utensils
- shaving only half your face
- growing a beard or shaving a beard off
- wearing outlandish makeup or wearing no makeup
- wearing a wig, hairpiece, or hat—or leaving your wig, hairpiece, or hat at home!

  Pretend you're:

- an immigrant who can't speak English and is trying to get directions to the train station, to buy a book, and to find a restaurant
- disabled and borrow a wheelchair to use for an hour
- blind and wear eyepatches under sunglasses for an hour
- a member of the opposite sex, when making decisions
- 30 years older or younger, and dress the part
- paralyzed; stay in bed for a day
- poor and broke; spend a day downtown with no cash or credit cards.

If you're less adventurous, try:

- wearing a winter suit in summertime or vice versa
- mixing stripes and checks
- taking your coffee black
- using the stairs instead of the elevator.

It may not be a momentous departure from your norm, but you need to break out of even small ruts.

Don't try to make sense out of what you might experience or learn at first. Just enjoy trying something new. Your left brain may proclaim the foolishness of it all, but your right brain will sing with delight and show you sights and wonders you never knew existed!

Your thinking tends to track your activities and your ways of looking at things. Therefore, to experience new and different perspectives, you have to try new and different things.

A child can do it

It's been said that we all start our lives as creative risk-takers. When you were a child you let your imagination have free rein. You created make-believe adventures, games, and creatures as freely as you breathed. You can still learn a lot about creativity from watching children play—and even more by playing along with them.

Take the time to play with children and let them do the leading! If they say the living room is a tropical jungle, offer to be a rubber tree. When expensive creative specialists gather round to work, they often start by playing with ideas—creating imaginary scenarios and impossible situations. They work by playing like children.

EXERCISE 19

Task: To brainstorm ideas about becoming more physically fit
Objectives: 1) To learn how to generate lots of ideas
            2) To become more creative

Go back to the end of Chapter 3 and review the problem you chose for practice there. Keep it handy for your second brainstorming activity. Your first attempt will be for fun and practice.

Gather five or six friends together for an evening for this exercise. You'll need some large pieces of paper (flip-chart paper is best), some felt pens, and a room to work in. Review the following rules of brainstorming with the group:

- The object is to generate as many ideas as possible
- Everybody has to contribute
- No idea is too trivial or silly

- Avoid regimented settings, such as sitting in rows or around a table
- Use free association and say whatever pops into your mind
- Choose a recorder to write down every idea
- Write the seed idea in the middle
- Record an idea beside the idea that inspired it (see below)
- Set a time limit (four or five minutes works well)
- Don't try to evaluate any ideas here. No logic is required. If someone says "ice cream" and someone else offers "rubber tree," don't ask why. Write it down.

Here's how your sheet might turn out if you start with the word "fitness."

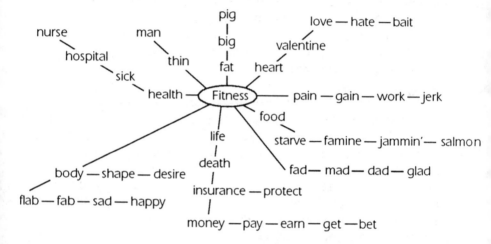

Now that you're all loosened up, try narrowing the focus a bit. This time you'll brainstorm ideas related to getting fit. How many ways are there to get fit? Use the same format as you did above. The result might look something like this:

Evaluation

You're learning that ideas are quite easy to generate. In one evening, you could possibly come up with dozens of ways to solve the small problem you identified earlier on. If you had previously thought of only one or two ways to get fit, you now have a lot more options.

⚷ KEY POINT Entrepreneurs practice generating lots of ideas

If you think ideas are rare, you're more likely to hang on to them whatever their actual value. Great ideas will also seem out of your reach—the obvious ones are already taken while the really revolutionary ideas are being sat on by mysterious corporate interests. It's a common misconception.

You've probably experienced this scenario. The after-dinner conversation turns to the subject of great ideas, such as a device that cuts automobile gas consumption in half (or eliminates the need for gasoline altogether by allowing engines to run on water). Or the talk is about a fertilizer that produces enormous vegetables, or a drug that eliminates the risk from smoking cigarettes—take your pick.

But, in a voice dripping with cynicism, the storyteller says that the government (or oil companies or grocery conglomerates or tobacco companies) have bought the rights to the idea and are sitting on it. And you can believe it because the story was told to the teller by a cousin who has a friend who's seen the device actually work! Heads shake knowingly, ruefully. "There's no point in trying something new," the diners agree. "Somebody's got all the good ideas locked up tight."

Things could be worse. You may know of someone who thought up a new board game and tried to duplicate the success of Trivial Pursuit. Maybe you know some inventors, Judy and Joe, who worked secretly in their basement for months, telling no one for fear their idea would be stolen. They put all their savings into preparing a prototype and, finally, burst out into the sunshine of reality to announce their idea to a waiting world, only to discover that nobody cared because there were dozens of new games Judy and Joe hadn't known existed that nobody cared about either. Every inventor in the world was trying to duplicate the success of Trivial Pursuit, which can only happen like that once. And Judy and Joe are left knowing they'll never try anything like that again. Which is a real pity. With a better knowledge of the role of ideas in the process of entrepreneurship, Judy and Joe might have turned their energies and resources to a viable venture.

Without the knowledge, discipline, and skills of entrepreneurship, an idea can be like a loose cannon ready to flatten the unwary, would-be entrepreneur. Too many people assume that if they just had one great idea, the rest would take care of itself.

Ideas without entrepreneurship are like one hand clapping

By now you'll know not to get depressed at these scenarios. But, you'll also know you can go wrong if you've never been taught to:

• test ideas for a proven market and viability
• work hard for a long time
• plan to raise adequate financing and be prepared for the worst-case scenario
• expect minimal financial returns at first
• back away if the idea doesn't appear viable
• distinguish inventing from entrepreneuring.

If invention is the key, what is the lock?

Have you ever tried inventing? Maybe you didn't invent a new fuel-injection system or a new type of heat-resistant plastic, but you may have come up with a better way to keep a door open on a hot day. Perhaps you accidentally added a new ingredient to a baking recipe and invented a new cookie. Whatever your invention, you probably thought it was special, and wondered if more people might feel the same way. Sometimes the idea seems so obvious, you're tempted to throw your life savings into it immediately. Before you go that far, meet some young entrepreneurs who might advise you to cool off a bit, first.

PRO FILE

Entrepreneurs: Wade Pugh and David Konduc

Enterprise: Chewter's Chocolates

Kelly Greville was sitting in a local tavern one evening, watching the waiters hustling trays of shot-glass-sized mixed liqueur drinks, called "shooters." She noticed that, after customers had knocked back the potions, some of them slipped the empty glasses into their pockets for souvenirs. "Hmmm," she mused. "What a waste. Too bad you couldn't eat the glass. These drinks are chocolaty, coffee-type stuff. What if the glasses were made out of chocolate? You could drink the drink and eat the glass! They'd be chewable shooters—Chewters!" Kelly raced home to tell her boyfriend, Wade Pugh, who, she says, almost "fell over backwards off his chair, he was so excited by the idea."

Wade and his friend, David Konduc, were born entrepreneurs, according to Kelly, and soon a partnership was formed to cash in on this great idea. "We thought we'd be rich in no time," says Wade, "but reality's not like that."

Although they were long on enthusiasm and optimism, none of the partners had any experience in chocolate production of any kind. Ditto for sales and marketing. They tried to get advice, but, because of their youth, the advice was lightly given. Nevertheless, they pressed on, making mistakes at every turn. They borrowed money based on incomplete planning; they bought the wrong equipment and the wrong chocolate and they worked long, hard hours. They sold some chocolate shot glasses, but it wasn't long before the original idea had given way to a product that sold even better: chocolate-covered rice cakes.

They now had contracts, but to fill them they'd have to mass-produce the cakes, and to do that, they had to design their own production process. With the help of an extraordinary plumber, they used existing knowledge of piping and assembly lines in an innovative way that had never been tried before. It worked.

Nine years after startup, Kelly and two other partners have gone on to other things. Wade and David have persisted and achieved some real success, although, according to Wade, "What we accomplished in five years could have been done in two and a half." Their products compete directly with those of the huge multinational candy conglomerates. Last year they did $1.2 million in sales, and this year they're headed for $2 million.

Their advice to would-be entrepreneurs: "Keep your day job. Learn something before you start. Plan ahead. Know everything you can about what you're producing."

 More than ideas, knowledge is the basis of entrepreneurship

Entrepreneurs and Inventors

As the young entrepreneurs above learned, it's one thing to invent something, and another to turn it into a viable venture. Inventors and entrepreneurs are really two different animals. Inventors get their thrills from perfecting a new gadget or gizmo, rather than from developing a business. Entrepreneurs excel at putting inventions to use. Inventors sometimes end up with nothing, while their inventions are marketed by someone else.

The photocopier, for example, sat on a shelf for years before Xerox bought the patent and took the process to market. One of the best-selling cars in history, the Chevrolet, was invented by a man named Chevrolet who sold out long before he could get rich from his creation. The Wright brothers made some money from the aircraft industry, but nothing compared to the billions made by Boeing or Airbus Industrie.

Inventions can earn their inventors tidy sums, but much of that money is often spent on patent lawsuits. Many people claim to have invented the telephone, or the parts that make up the phone. Alexander Bell fought hard to establish his patent and it's his name we now associate with the invention. Thomas Edison, credited with inventing the light bulb, competed with many inventors of his day, some of whom claimed to have been the first to make a working light bulb.

Do you know who invented television, radio, the radial tire, or the transistor? Likely not. But do you recognize the names of Sony, Panasonic, Goodyear, and RCA? They may not have invented the original concept or prototypes of the products they sell, but they were the innovators who actually made these products available to millions of consumers. Their contribution was more entrepreneurship than invention.

In some cases, inventors are able to innovate after the fact. For them, perseverance pays off when they find a market for their invention. In Chapter 3 you learned that a product in search of a market often dies a slow death. Here's a story about three physicists whose invention cheated death.

PRO FILE

Entrepreneurs: Gary Albach, Dave Camm, and Steve Richards

Enterprise: Vortek Industries Ltd.

Anyone who has witnessed a bolt of lightning or seen an arc-welder in operation knows that electrical arcs produce very bright light. This simple fact intrigued three academic physicists who were conducting not-so-simple post-doctoral research in plasma physics when they invented the world's brightest artificial light.

"Physicists have known for some years that an electrical arc could be made to produce a very bright light," explains Gary Albach. "But because such an arc would generate tremendous heat, no one had invented a way of preventing it from melting whatever contained it. Our theory solved that problem."

Their theory went like this: the lamp they designed would use 100,000 watts of electricity, which would be arced between two specially designed tungsten tips. To dissipate the heat (twice the temperature of the sun's surface), the arc would be induced through a quartz tube, and held in the center, or vortex, of a low-pressure field generated by water swirling through the tube at high pressure. In effect, the water would form a heat-absorbing wall between the arc and the tube. The resulting light would be the most powerful in the world—capable of lighting 10 soccer fields simultaneously. They were so convinced that their invention would work that they obtained the rights to the research, quit their jobs, and started Vortek, manufacturer of the world's brightest light bulbs.

Their invention worked. They had created the world's brightest artificial light source. Unfortunately, they forgot to check whether anyone actually wanted or needed such a bright light.

"We really did everything backwards," says Gary, who took over the business side of the company.

"We had read books on business plans and thought we knew what we were doing, but in the end, we had a solution in search of a problem." Fortunately for Vortek, they had two solutions. Along with the bright light, their lamp also produced tremendous heat—heat that could be focused and controlled.

Today, Vortek is alive and thriving. Gary, Dave, and Steve have sold dozens of lamps (each costing up to $200,000), some as big as 300,000 watts, all to customers who needed heat, not light. Their customers have included companies in the metals-hardening industry and NASA, where their lamp has been used to heat-test shuttle rocket nozzles.

The three physicists at Vortek learned the difference between invention and innovation in the world of high technology. But the same principles apply to low technology.

The everyday innovator

What uses have you found for empty plastic containers? Clothespins? Popcorn? Cut the top off plastic bleach bottles and you have a useful funnel. Clothespins can be used to seal leftover bags of potato chips. Popcorn is being used as environmentally friendly filler for packaging. When you find a new use for an old product, you're an innovator. And when you find lots of people to buy and use your innovation, you're an entrepreneur.

Part-time inventors often have grand plans in mind as they toil away on new gadgets or widgets. But inventing is a routine activity for professional inventors, who are usually called industrial or product designers. Most of the products you see around you were designed or invented by professionals.

If you have an idea for a new device or product, you'd be well advised to seek out one of these professional designers for help. An industrial designer doesn't work for free. But if you want your idea thoroughly evaluated and perfected, your money will be well spent on their professional advice.

To be a good industrial designer, you have to enjoy inventing. But you also have to be an engineer, visionary, mechanic, and an artist. It wouldn't do to make something that worked but was so ugly that no one would want it. Similarly, it doesn't make sense to make something that's pleasing to look at, but not functional. Finally, it may cost you a considerable amount of money to find out that something just won't work at all. But it's far better to find out at the inventing stage than at the manufacturing or marketing part of the venture.

If you recall Ron Foxcroft's Fox 40 whistle from Chapter 2, you'll remember that he hired a professional product designer to come up with a pea-less whistle. The person he hired was Chuck Shepherd. Entrepreneurs can learn a lot from Chuck.

PRO FILE

Product Designer: Chuck Shepherd

Unofficial Mission: To save entrepreneurs from themselves

"People come to me and say, 'I have five great ideas. I want to do all of them over the next year.' I say, 'Pick the simplest one and be prepared to commit five years of your life to it,'" says Chuck. He should know, because he worked more than three years designing a whistle that didn't have a pea in it. It sounds simple, but nothing is simple, according to Chuck, who makes it his business to find simpler and better ways of making things. "It wasn't just a matter of making a whistle that would work. I had to make a whistle that looked and felt familiar to referees and to others who use whistles all the time, and it's not easy to please those people," says Chuck. "They tend to find things not to like. For example, they'd find it too big, too small, too loud, or too light, and so on."

"It makes all the difference in the world when the entrepreneur—the person with the idea— is working in his or her own area of expertise. For example, if a nurse comes to me with an idea related to health care, it's a lot better than someone just dreaming up an idea for a new automobile muffler when they know nothing about cars and sound control," Chuck advises.

It helped that Chuck's client, Ron Foxcroft, is a skilled entrepreneur. As well as being a successful businessperson, Ron is a professional referee himself, and he was trying to solve a problem that he and other referees had always had: the pea-whistle could jam if it was overblown. Not only was Ron Chuck's client, but he also represented the whistle's target market.

It took three years and more than $150,000 to produce a final prototype whistle. Then came more problem solving and more refinement— "thousandths of an

---

inch here and there," says Chuck—before the final product was approved for mass production. Ron and Chuck worked with Dan Bruno, an injection mold specialist who oversaw the production start-up, and through all this, Ron championed the product to anybody who would listen.

The Fox 40 is a tremendous success, but according to Chuck Shepherd, most ideas aren't viable, in spite of how enthusiastic their creators might be. The success of the Fox 40 whistle was possible because the best people directed their talents and skills to the simplest and best possible, clearly defined entrepreneurial idea.

Chuck suggests finding a reputable designer through a design association, government agency, design school, or college. "Don't hesitate to ask questions regarding the designer's background and confirm his or her experience in your area of interest," he says.

Chuck also advises caution when choosing from the endless ranks of companies who offer services relating to licensing your product. "While some offer legitimate services at reasonable costs, others are out-and-out scam artists who will lead you by the hand into near-bankruptcy."

"Patents are particularly important when it comes to licensing arrangements," says Chuck. "Entrepreneurs are sometimes slow off the mark when it comes to patenting. They're also often overly suspicious about people stealing their ideas. Ideas are actually rarely stolen. People have little to fear in confiding their ideas to reputable product designers or patent agents."

 10% of something is better than 100% of nothing

Really great ideas aren't usually earthshaking. In fact, totally new products are extremely rare. Most new ideas involve making existing things better, more efficient, smaller, or larger. These changes are called innovations. When entrepreneurs innovate, they actually put an idea to use. It can be a new way of doing or making things, and sometimes it seems amazing that some obvious improvements take so long.

Check your oil?

Take motor oil containers, for example. At one time, engine oil for cars and trucks could only be purchased in bulk—by the barrel or pail. Engines were messy things and one could expect to get a little greasy when servicing them. But, as the trend to more convenient products swept through society, oil became available in premeasured metal quart or liter containers. Auto drivers could now add their own oil as needed, but they still had to get it out of the can and into the engine. Can openers, spouts, and funnels appeared in all varieties and designs—each promising to transfer the oil to the engine without spilling and each failing to greater or lesser degrees. Although variety abounded, efficiency stalled.

Meanwhile, plastic containers became the popular choice for soaps, soft drinks, and other liquids. After a remarkably long time, they found their way around lubricating oil. The can opener was banished. Just unscrew the cap and pour the oil—all over your hands, around the filler cap and over the hot exhaust manifold. Some oil even found its way into the engine. What was going on here? Where was the improvement? Without funnels, the whole process was just as messy as before!

When it finally appeared, the sensible oil container looked so obvious. Its only innovative feature was a slightly elongated pouring spout. The earth didn't shake, but heads did. Why, wondered consumers, did it take so long just to fashion a plastic container with a funnel, or spout, as part of its design? All that was required was a slightly longer neck, and goodbye to metal funnels, spouts, and splattered clothing. Why, indeed?

Maybe it's because there aren't enough entrepreneurs around. What bugs you? Are you on the lookout for products that need improvement? It's easier to spot opportunities for innovation if you know how to identify previous innovative improvements.

EXERCISE 20

Task: To identify innovations in everyday products
Objective: To learn about the role innovation plays in daily life

You won't have to go far to do this exercise. Kitchens are good places to look for innovation. Explore your kitchen. What products can you find that represent innovative improvements over their predecessors? The first few suggestions should get you started:

PRODUCT	ONCE WAS	WHICH ONCE WAS	WHICH ONCE WAS
Electric carving knife	Manual carving knife	Hunting knife	Flint knife
Electric stove	Wood stove	Fireplace	Open fire

Now, try finding small innovations in a common everyday object. Describe each version and what it does better. For example, let's look at footwear.

PRODUCT	HOW BETTER?
Rawhide moccasin	Protects bare feet from injury, allows freer movement
Heavy leather sole	More protection, longer wear
Polished leather shoe	Appeals to fashion
Arch support	Greater comfort, less fatigue
Eyelets, laced shoe	Easier lacing
Canvas shoe	Lighter, cheaper
Rubber shoe	Waterproof, durable
Running shoe	Lighter, better traction
Molded shape	Greater comfort and support; less fatigue
High-heeled shoe	Fashion appeal
Orthopedic shoe	Therapeutic
Riding boot	Protects rider from elements
Hip-wading boot	Keeps legs and thighs dry while fishing
Ballet slipper	Allows technical dance feats

Try the same exercise again, applying it to writing tools, underwear, bicycles, and telephones.

PRODUCT	HOW BETTER?
_____	_____
_____	_____
_____	_____
_____	_____
_____	_____
_____	_____

Evaluation

You're learning that the things we use in everyday life reflect continuous innovation. By noticing the importance of what appear to be minor changes and improvements in everyday products, you'll be better able to recognize where small improvements are needed. Then you'll learn to set aside large, unwieldy ideas in favor of small, more manageable ones.

 Entrepreneurs spot products that trail technology

Pardon me, is this the end of the line?

Innovative products are important, but you can find innovation in the way society functions, too. Do you remember always choosing the wrong line when you lined up at the bank? You'd eye the lines to see which was short-est and choose that one. Immediately the other lines would begin to shorten. You'd jump to another one just as the customer ahead of you began a 15-minute transaction. In frustration, you'd see satisfied customers, who had been behind you, now leaving.

Have you noticed that this scenario doesn't happen any more? Now, there is only one mazelike line and customers are led efficiently, one by one, to the next available teller. It works. This simple innovative way of arranging lines has saved customers' time and reduced some of the stress of lining up.

Your call has been forwarded to a computer chip

As you learned in the last chapter, nothing has produced more opportunities than technological change. New technology has ushered in the age of infor-mation, which, in turn, has spun off innovations affecting aspects of our daily lives. Telephone calls are answered by electronic machines. Television "listens" to us when we use interactive devices, such as video games and public information terminals. More innovative ideas appear each day, as aspects of new technology are mixed and matched.

When you read the bank story above, you may have thought, "But I don't use banks any more; I use cash machines." The cash machine, or instant teller, is an example of innovation involving the application of exist-ing technologies in new ways.

The little brown strip of magnetic tape on the back of your bank card is old technology. The computer chip has been around for quite some time, too, as has the capability of sending digital information over phone lines. Mechanical devices that count and dispense money are nothing new, either. What is innovative is the way these technologies are put together.

Insert your bank card and a mechanical motor pulls it into a slot. There a magnetic audio playback head reads the brown tape, which contains digital information that identifies you and your account number. A video screen dis-plays the transaction. Your bank account is accessed through a telephone line and you are asked to enter your code. A simple logic circuit processes your code, and a computer, satisfied that you are who you say you are, allows you to deposit or withdraw money from your account. When you request cash, a simple calculator balances your account; a printer prints a receipt and a mechanical device dispenses your cash.

You've likely only started using these machines within the past few years, but that little brown strip has been part of your credit card for at least 20 years! How long have bar codes been part of products labels? How long did Touch Tone telephones have the * and # symbols before we actually started to use them? For years and years. The ideas that make call forward-ing, electronic answering machines, bar-code pricing, and instant cash-dis-

market and what they're used for. But implementation takes time. It takes decades, in some cases, to align all the necessary ingredients.

Growing concern about the quality of our natural environment has opened windows of opportunities in many areas, but none are so promising as in environmental technology, as Cody Slater found.

PRO FILE

Entrepreneur: Cody Slater

Enterprise: B & W Technologies

One summer, Cody Slater took a break from his undergraduate studies in physics to travel and explore. Ironically, he made his greatest discovery in his own home turf, which is known for its rich oil and gas industry.

Cody knew his way around the gas fields and their dangers. Like most people in his region, he read about accidents involving gas workers and the dreaded sour gas that can kill with one sniff. In a typical tragic incident, a pair of gas workers would arrive at the site of a gas well to check and maintain the installation, which is usually housed in a small building called a shack. The first worker would enter the shack and, before he could even cry out, he'd be killed by the deadly, odorless fumes. His partner, curious about what his buddy was doing, would enter the shack as well, doubling the tragedy.

Of course, gas companies employed complex technological detection devices that were supposed to provide an early warning of the presence of sour gas. But Cody discovered that these devices were large, cumbersome, and technologically outdated. They also failed regularly.

Cody recognized opportunity. "I think of myself as an innovator," he says, "which is different from an inventor. Rather than inventing new technology, I try to use existing technology in new ways."

He decided to use the rest of his summer holidays to devise a gas-detecting device that could do the job better. He studied existing technology and began to rework it in a few key ways: He miniaturized the electronic unit from one that covered a whole wall to one the size of a tissue box; he upgraded the quality so that it could withstand extremes of temperature and humidity; he powered it with solar energy so that it wouldn't be subject to electrical failures and he built in a miniature transmitting unit that reported to a central receiver. He called it the Rig Rat.

Three years later, Cody Slater had still not completed his physics degree. He was too busy with his new company, B & W Technologies, which had grown quickly to more than 30 employees. Cody's Rig Rat worked, and it could survive extreme temperatures and operating conditions. On one occasion, a shack burned to the ground and the Rig Rat was found, charred and partly melted in the debris, but still functioning perfectly. The gas industry was quick to embrace Cody's new device and he carefully scrutinized potential partners and regularly entertained offers of venture capital.

Innovation begets innovation and soon Cody's Rig Rat found new applications. Because it could be placed inexpensively at remote locations, a major oil company chose the Rig Rat over all competitors to save its multibillion-dollar pipeline. Environmentalists and property owners demanded that gas detectors be placed at regular intervals along the length of the pipeline before they would allow it to go into operation.

Today, Cody is developing devices that will detect and vent radon gas in homes, and he has expanded his industrial product line as well.

"I believe that we are seeing just the beginning of the revolution in environmental technology," says Cody. "Environmental technology today is where consumer electronics was 25 years ago, and the companies that are involved on the cutting edge are going to be the Sonys and Panasonics of the future."

The Tug of War: Innovation and Resistance to Change

Just as Cody Slater uses existing technology in innovative ways to link gas fields and pipelines to a central receiver, many of today's innovators are using existing information and communication to link and shrink the world of the commuter.

Fifty years ago, commuters drove cars, walked, or rode streetcars or buses to office buildings, where they sat in row upon row of desks, sorting paper reports and orders. They typed up new reports, using layers of carbon paper to produce copies of the original. Telephones, messengers, and the postal service carried the bulk of interoffice communications. Products and services moved at the speed of trains, trucks, and ships.

In spite of fax machines, cellular phones, and computer networks, most people still take subways, buses, and automobiles to work. The expressways are still choked with thousands of cars every morning, each heading to a central office somewhere. Instead of typewriters, most desks now sport computer terminals. Carbon paper has been replaced by photocopiers that copy and collate. Workers access information through computer networks via phone lines, faxes, and modems. Courier services are still prospering and everyone still uses the post office for much of their communications.

But more and more commuters are asking themselves, "Why do I have to leave my home, where I have a computer, modem, fax machine, and phone, to go to an office to use a computer, modem, fax machine, and phone?" For no good reason, it appears, as thousands of office workers are parking their cars and staying home—to work.

Like the cash machine, the technology that allows you to do the same work at home as you might do at an office has been around for some time. Why, then, is it taking so long to catch on? The answer is related to the discussion of ruts and habits earlier in this chapter. To be innovative, you have to change your way of looking at and doing things.

By now, you'll be more favorably disposed to change. You understand that change is only as threatening as you choose to see it. But, most people don't like change. They resist it.

If you examine all the benefits of working from your own home, the list might look like this:

- No more commuting, which means:
  - more time to do other things (from a half hour to more than four hours for some people)
  - one or two automobiles can be eliminated, which, in turn, means
    - reduced transportation costs
    - reduced risk from accidents
    - more garage space
    - less automobile pollution
    - less traffic congestion on streets and expressways
  - less worry about the weather, road conditions, exposure
  - fewer restaurant meals

- No need to look the part, which means:
  - reduced wardrobe costs
  - fewer worries about looking right
  - more comfort by eliminating restrictive suits, ties, and pantyhose

- Less contact with people and office environment, which means:
  - reduced risk of catching or passing on communicable diseases
  - less exposure to stale office air
  - reduced exposure to sexual harassment, office politics

- Work becomes self-directed, which means:
  - you can work at your own pace, as long as the job gets done
  - you can set your own hours—work in the middle of the night, if you prefer
  - fewer physical interruptions, except the phone
  - no boss looking over your shoulder
  - you take more control of your own life

- increased overall privacy
- Employers can cut overhead costs, reducing or eliminating:
  - office and parking space
  - snack service, lunchrooms
  - travel subsidies
  - supervisory staff.

For these reasons, growing numbers of people have opted out of the commuter rut. But many people are resisting the trend.

EXERCISE 21

Task: To identify possible resistance to working from your own home
Objective: To learn about resistance to change

List some reasons why the various groups identified below might resist the practice of working at home, or "telecommuting," as it's sometimes called. Some examples are provided to help you.

RESISTER	REASONS TO RESIST
Employers	Loss of direct personal control over employees
Middle managers	Supervisory jobs may disappear
Employees	May not be computer-literate
Auto industry	

RESISTER   **REASONS TO RESIST**

_____

_____

_____

_____

Oil and gas industry_____

_____

_____

_____

_____

_____

Day-care industry_____

_____

_____

_____

_____

_____

Children and spouses   Work invades home life_____

_____

_____

_____

_____

Food service industry_____

_____

_____

_____

Fashion industry_____

_____

_____

_____

_____

▶ ▶ ▶ ▶▶▶▶▶

RESISTER	REASONS TO RESIST
Commercial realtors	
Civic governments	Tax base may be eroded in business districts
Labor unions	May fear exploitation of workers

Evaluation

As usual, there are lots of different right answers. Here are some explanations of why these groups might resist the home office trend.

Employers: May fear losing some control over employees and losing personal interaction; may not trust employees to do work; may fear less power; may fear using the new technologies.

Middle managers: May fear their jobs becoming redundant; may fear losing power and influence.

Employees: May fear losing company benefits; may not wish to lose companionship of fellow employees; may enjoy commuting and networking; may need the daily assistance of fellow workers; may need personal reassurance of jobs well done; may not want to spend more time with family; may not have a room at home to work in; may not feel confident operating a computer, modem, or fax machine; may need to be motivated by others to work.

Auto industry: May fear diminished market and reduced sales.

Petroleum industry: May fear reduced gasoline, oil, and maintenance sales.

Day care industry: May fear loss of clientele.

Children and spouses: May not be able to adjust to home worker; may fear getting in the way; may not want to give up space, telephone time, and privacy.

Food service industry: May fear loss of clientele for lunches.

Fashion industry: May fear loss of sales of business attire.

Commercial realtors: May fear empty office buildings and loss of new opportunities to develop commercial space.

Civic governments: May fear commercial rezoning and changing tax bases.

Labor unions: May fear loss of control over members and employers; may fear exploitation of workers by employers; may fear loss of protected jobs to piecework contracts.

Every innovation meets resistance, no matter how apparently obvious its improvements might seem. As you focus on your entrepreneurial idea, you may become overly optimistic about how your innovative product or service will be received in the marketplace. It's important that you know that resistance will come and that it may be fierce. You also need to know where the resistance will come from, and why, so that you can adjust your startup and marketing strategy to overcome that resistance.

Try one more exercise, just to make sure you're becoming more sensitive to who the naysayers might be and why they will oppose you so much. See if you can identify what groups might have been major opponents of these well-known innovations:

INNOVATION	RESISTERS
The automobile	
Electric light	
Licensed medical doctors	
Consumer organizations	
Licensed lawyers	
Self-serve gasoline stations	
The nicotine patch for smokers	
Licensed midwives	
Organic farming	
Television	

 Entrepreneurs anticipate resistance and work hard to overcome it

It's your turn

Using the fitness example from the end of Chapter 3, you learned how to brainstorm lots of ideas in the first exercise in this chapter. Through that exercise, you learned that ideas aren't rare and that it's quite easy to identify opportunities.

Next, you learned how to distinguish between inventing and innovating and how to identify resistance to innovation. You've had a chance to practice with sample ideas that were provided for you, but now it's time to evaluate your very own innovative idea. By now, you're likely champing at the bit to get at it. Remember, it doesn't have to be earthshaking. In fact, it's better if it's a small, manageable, and doable improvement.

Evaluating Your Idea

It's time to find out whether your idea can stand some scrutiny. The main purpose of this exercise is to show you that there's more to establishing a viable idea than just dreaming it up. You'll have to do your research first, and that might take some time. In the example looked at in this exercise, you'd study the food service industry in general and natural food restaurants in particular. You'll need to do some informal market research, at least—simply asking people what they think of your idea would be a start. The best way to get this information is to talk to someone who is in this business already.

EXERCISE 22

Task: To evaluate my own entrepreneurial idea
Objective: To set the stage for my venture

1. What is my opportunity?

Start by writing down the opportunity you'll be addressing with your idea. Let's say you see the trend to natural foods as an opportunity to exploit a growing need for natural foods. First, you'll have to be clear that there really is an opportunity in the natural food industry. Write down your opportunity and then check off each of the points of evaluation, to make sure you're clear about the viability of your opportunity.

My Opportunity: _____

My research has proven that the problem is (you should be able to check each one):

- ☐ Real
- ☐ Widespread
- ☐ Important to others
- ☐ Currently being under-addressed or improperly addressed
- ☐ Clearly defined
- ☐ Within my area of expertise or potential expertise
- ☐ The best one I can find
- ☐ An area I will enjoy working in
- ☐ A window of opportunity for me

2. What is my general idea?

Next you have to brainstorm as many ideas as possible that could address your opportunity. If, for example, you see the trend to natural foods as an opportunity that's perfect for you, you need to come up with as many ways of exploiting that opportunity as possible. Will you grow organic food, sell wholesale or retail produce, open a restaurant, or test organic food for contaminants? Each of these possibilities represents a general idea.

My general idea is: _____

_____

_____

_____

3. What is my specific idea?

Once you've identified the best idea (let's say it's a restaurant), list all the types of restaurants you might consider, such as fast-food, upscale, large, small, urban, rural, with a large or small menu. Each of these decisions has to take into account your skills, resources, knowledge, and ambition. A large restaurant featuring an extensive menu will require more skill and resources and involve more risk. If you have restaurant experience, you may be able to begin on a large scale, otherwise you'd be wise to start small.

A specific idea might look like this: A 50-seat diner located near the local college, featuring an inexpensive, fast-food vegetarian menu; the decor is railroad dining-car, art deco; the diner will be open 24 hours a day, 365 days a year, and the staff will wear 1950s uniforms.

Write down your specific idea, refining and qualifying it as much as possible.

My specific idea is: _____

_____

_____

_____

_____

_____

4. Who is my specific market?

You'll have to know exactly who your customers will be, so you can tailor your idea to them. An example of a specific market for the diner idea would be: The primary market is vegetarian or health-conscious students or people between the ages of 16 and 25 with low income who live in the immediate vicinity of the diner and are currently being served by part of the menu in a larger restaurant halfway across town. The secondary market is 25- to 45-year-old health-conscious urban professionals. Write down your specific market.

My specific market is: _____

_____

_____

_____

5. How can I evaluate my specific idea?

To help evaluate your idea, read the following detailed questions, which the entrepreneur who's planning the vegetarian diner should answer.

a) Do I have knowledge of, or can I identify a member of my team who has knowledge of:
  - health food?
  - the restaurant business?
  - my target market?
  - zoning restrictions?
  - the number, type, location, and success of competitors?
  - health regulations?
  - inventory control?
  - advertising venues in the community?

b) Do I know how much it will cost me to open the restaurant?
  - How much can I expect to gross in the first year?
  - How many employees will I need, where will I find them, and how much will I pay them?
  - Can I raise the necessary financial resources?

c) Am I prepared to work the kind of hours it will take to:
  - prepare a business plan?
  - build a team?
  - find and renovate a suitable location?
  - locate, train, and supervise my employees?
  - research and establish my supply network?
  - deal with insurance companies, supply shortages, surpluses, and local bylaws?
  - stay open six or seven days per week?

d) Is my idea innovative? How?

e) Has my idea been tried before? Successfully? Unsuccessfully? Can I explain why it was either successful or unsuccessful?

f) Could someone else copy my idea, using greater resources than I have? Easily?

g) Do I know what a worst-case scenario would look like? Can I, or would I be willing to, survive it?

h) Do my spouse and family agree with everything I have indicated above? Are they willing to support me in my venture?

Now evaluate your specific idea by answering the following questions as they relate to it.

1. Do I have sufficient knowledge about this type of venture? _____

2. If not, am I willing and able to learn what I need to know? _____

3. How much it will cost me to start this venture? _____

4. How much can I expect to gross in the first year? _____

5. How many employees will I need? _____
Where will I find them? _____
How much will I pay them? _____

6. Can I raise the necessary financial resources? _____

7. Am I prepared to work the kind of hours it will take to:
- prepare a business plan? _____
- build a team? _____
- find and renovate a suitable location? _____
- locate, train, and supervise employees? _____
- research and establish my supply network? _____
- deal with insurance companies and local bylaws? _____
- deal with supply shortages and surpluses? _____

8. How is my idea innovative? _____
_____
_____
_____
_____

9. Has my idea been tried before? _____
Successfully? _____
Unsuccessfully? _____

10. Why was it either successful or unsuccessful? _____
_____
_____
_____
_____
_____

Evaluation

How does your idea stack up? Has it begun to lose some of its initial appeal? If so, take another good hard look at it; it will never be as cheap to abandon it as it is now. Or does it appear more attractive than ever? Then, carry on. Are you a little frightened about what you're getting yourself into? If so, good. Confidence is important, but over-confidence can be life-threatening. Even highly skilled musicians and performers get nervous before important engagements. It's part of the thrill.

A proven innovative idea will be the basis of the venture you're going to learn to build in the next chapter. But, first, here's a summary of the key points from Chapter 4.

KEY POINT **Summary**

Entrepreneurs practice generating lots of ideas
Ideas without entrepreneurship are like one hand clapping
More than ideas, knowledge is the basis of entrepreneurship
10% of something is better than 100% of nothing
Entrepreneurs spot products that trail technology
Entrepreneurs anticipate resistance and work hard to overcome it

CHAPTER 5

Getting Started

*The secret of
getting ahead is
getting started*

🔖 OLD SAYING

Once you've identified your best idea and found that it could survive an evaluation process like the one at the end of Chapter 4, you have to make a decision: Are you going to do something with this idea, or are you going to practice finding other opportunities and continue brainstorming more ideas? If you're not sure, you're better off choosing the latter. If you are sure, it's time to take the next step. It's time to create a venture around your idea.

Building a venture involves finding money to get started, developing prototypes, working with people, and trying to make money. It's not child's play. You're going to have to work hard. You're going to have to plan.

Different ventures start in different ways. Getting started might mean going into production in one case, and working on a venture plan in another. Nevertheless, planning is part of getting any venture started. This chapter is largely about why planning is important and how you can use your existing skills to get started on planning your venture. It's about:

• how people like you actually got started
• the purpose of planning
• how to prepare a venture plan
• how first-time entrepreneurs usually raise money
• why prototypes are important
• the importance of team building
• how to work with partners.

Having done the last exercise in Chapter 4, you'll be happy to know you've already done much of what's involved in planning your venture.

Be Prepared

You already know lots about planning. Almost everyone does. Organization and planning go hand in hand. But, most of us have had to learn planning the hard way. No doubt you've gone to the hardware store to buy a hammer, only to return home and discover that you still need nails. After a while, you discover the merits of making shopping lists. Planning saves you time and money. The more money and less time you have to lose, the more planning is important.

Why a venture plan?

Planning your venture is no different from planning your life. You wouldn't buy a car or house you couldn't afford, so why would you start a venture you couldn't afford? In short, if you've already learned how to set priorities, how to manage money, and how to be efficient in your everyday activities, you can handle a venture plan.

A venture plan is simply a description of what your venture is about: what you plan to do, why you plan to do it, who will help you, and how and when you'll start and run your venture. You'll need a venture plan to convince other people that you'll be successful. You'll also need it to help keep yourself organized.

A venture plan is slightly different from a business plan. Not all businesses are new and innovative and, as you learned in Chapter 1, not all businesspeople are entrepreneurs. In fact, some businesses, such as franchises, are set up to be exact copies of other businesses. But if you're an entrepreneur, you're trying something new.

That said, business and venture plans look much the same—on the surface, at least. In their incomplete state, they present page after page of blanks for you to fill in. They use words such as: proprietorship, market analysis, equity, economic climate, liability, net income, and cash flow. (If you're not familiar with these terms, turn to "Business Lingo" on page 195 for some simple, straightforward definitions.)

You're being encouraged to take risks in this book, so it's important to make sure that such encouragement isn't irresponsible. As much as you can determine, you should know that your idea has a good chance of succeeding before you commit your time and resources to it.

Model plans and the real world of entrepreneurs

If ever there was a group who embodied the old saying, "Do as I say, not as I do," it's entrepreneurs. With one voice, they chant, "Make sure you know what you're getting into! Plan!" But, wait a minute! Most of them didn't know what they were getting into. They didn't plan. And although they suffered the consequences, they did get started and they don't regret becoming entrepreneurs. You should learn from their mistakes, but you shouldn't be daunted by them.

 It's important to plan, but it's more important to take that first step

It's time you met the person who's writing this book. I didn't do all the planning for my first venture that I'm asking you to do, but I wish I had. Here's how I got started.

Entrepreneurs: Jim Lang and Mary Ackroyd

Enterprises: Lang & Ackroyd Band; Little Johnny Records; Lang & Ackroyd Productions & Consulting

I wasn't born an entrepreneur. I don't think anyone is—unless everyone is. Like most people I tried to take an established career path, first as an academic (mostly philosophy, some English, and a teaching diploma) and then in government, as a youth worker. I was always trying to find a life that offered the kind of freedom and meaning my generation had come to believe was a birthright. I wasn't trying to be different, as my father suggested with some disapproval; I was just trying to find the life that was right for me.

I think I became an entrepreneur when I decided to quit trying to find meaning in jobs that were defined for me and, for the first time, defined a job for myself. I simply asked myself what I really liked to do, instead of what I thought I ought to do.

The answer was right in my face. I shelved my college degrees and diplomas, bought a new guitar and, with my new life-partner and kindred spirit, Mary Ackroyd, started to carve a niche in the music business.

We weren't good entrepreneurs or good musicians at the start. But Mary, who was a budding fiddle player, and I practiced hard, and I can still remember counting our pay—in cash—after our first week of work. It was an intoxicating experience. This was our own business and our own idea and the cash was proof that we were on the right track. We hired a couple of backup musicians to flesh out the act and we hit the road.

The Lang & Ackroyd Band

If you're diligent, as we mostly were, the music business provides an excellent course in entrepreneurship. Nothing builds—or tests—self-confidence like standing up in front of a big room full of strangers and singing them a song that they'll either love, hate, or ignore completely. Of course, the more skilled you are, the more self-confidence you'll have and the louder the audience will applaud—and the more you'll get paid.

In the music business, to a large extent, the process is also the product. Your show is your product and, if people like it, they stay and spend money. Audience feedback is immediate, and it forms the basis upon which you set your prices. If the feedback is negative, you change your approach, tunes, musicians, or venues. When the show's over, there's no arguing with the cash register—it never lies. Good sales = good band, viable venture.

▶ ▶ ▶ ▶▶▶▶▶

Apart from those skills directly related to the music business, we learned how to hire, fire, encourage, motivate, and manage employees; communicate (hold the attention of an audience); evaluate a market (what did people want to hear?); adjust the product to that market (learn to play what they want to hear); promote, advertise, and hustle contracts; price the product; delegate responsibility to agents, promoters, record producers, and fellow musicians; and plan for growth by staying on top of trends, chasing bigger markets, and upgrading equipment. We also learned to deal with daily problems, from musicians who fail to show up, to surviving New Year's Eve with laryngitis.

We didn't think of it in those terms, but we were innovators. Our show was different—we discovered we had a star fiddle player in Mary, who electrified audiences. We deliberately toured the hot spots, where the newest trends were emerging, and we were often on the cutting edge of the latest sounds. Sometimes we were too far ahead; we found that jumping the gun on a trend can be just as fruitless as missing the trend completely. We always used professional booking agencies and paid our bills. We even paid severance to fired employees, which may not sound innovative, but it is in the music business. Finally, we had a normal life on the road, complete with comfortable travel trailers. After our son was born, we even hired a nanny who accompanied us on the road.

We had made a few recordings that we enjoyed hearing and playing, but when audiences kept asking for an instrumental album, we decided to do one. We took our savings, hesitated for a moment as we realized we could also use that money to put a down payment on a house, and jumped in. This was no time to lose confidence.

Little Johnny Records

Our venture was fully capitalized at startup. We knew there was a niche market for our album and that most of our customers were probably older rather than younger. But, we had no idea how many of them were out there, and never bothered trying to find out.

We manufactured the smallest number of records and tapes that would take advantage of the biggest price break (1,000 units of each). But we spent too much for the album covers and too little on recording what they contained.

We distributed through television advertising and direct-mail campaigns, which we assumed would work, because they seemed to work for other record companies, even though we had no proof of that. We knew that there were no other fiddle and guitar albums being sold that way. But we never checked to see if any were currently in the works.

We hired amateurs to make our television commercial (thinking "how difficult can it be?") and paid far too much for what became a truly forgettable commercial. We set up phone lines and television P.I. deals. (P.I.

means you pay a percentage of each item sold in return for running your commercial; I was a sheep to be shorn by one or two TV stations.)

We bought packaging without weighing it to see what the postage would cost to mail it. We accepted CODs, which greatly increased overhead costs, and did our own shipping, which reduced costs.

To our amazement, we sold almost all our inventory and actually broke even, which we considered a runaway success under the circumstances.

The day our P.I. contracts were up, a huge competitor brought out a similar album, which, two months earlier, would have blown us out of the water. Fortunately, we escaped before that could happen. Little Johnny Records had a little planning and a lot of luck.

Enter Lang & Ackroyd Productions & Consulting

During the Little Johnny Records venture, the strain of parenthood, direct sales, and the grind of the road began to take its toll. It wasn't that we were disillusioned or felt unsuccessful. We just felt it was time for a change. When we decided to change directions, as always, our personal lives came first. I dusted off my teaching certificate and looked for a day job.

I didn't realize then that a few years of teaching would lead to a whole new set of ventures. In the classroom, I saw that the lessons of entrepreneurship could be used to help students make the transition from school to the workplace. There appeared to be a clear need for entrepreneurship education, and I felt television would be the best medium to help deliver it. And Lang & Ackroyd Productions & Consulting was born.

I turned my experience in show business and education to producing educational television. Not suprisingly the first series Lang & Ackroyd produced was called "Entrepreneurship: The Spirit of Adventure." Instead of singing tunes in clubs, I now sing the praises of entrepreneurship at conferences and workshops. It's all come together quite nicely.

 Nobody does it exactly right the first time or every time

Many entrepreneurs jump into ventures unprepared, as Mary and I did when we sank our savings into Little Johnny Records without doing any market research. Often they survive. But thorough planning is the best way to reduce and manage risk. Today, I'm a more skilled entrepreneur and I plan my ventures much more carefully. I encourage you to do likewise. See the appendix at the back of the book, page 197, for a sample venture plan that shows just the kind of planning you need to do.

Will Your Venture Need a Prototype?

Many ventures require prototypes. You may be trying to market a new fly swatter, for example, or a coffee mug for use in a car, or a new piece of exercise equipment. If your venture involves a new product or service, you'll need to demonstrate how it works before anyone will buy it or invest in it. Knowing it will work in theory just isn't good enough.

Remember Ron Foxcroft's whistle? It took three years and $150,000 to produce a working prototype. But he used the prototype to prove to his potential buyers that the thing would actually work. His prototype costs represent about 1% of his astonishingly successful sales so far. You should do so well. Other inventions can take longer than that. So if you're planning on introducing a product that will require injection molds or factory jigs, be prepared for considerable startup costs. A working prototype is essential if you're going to sell your product and you may have to borrow quite a bit of money just to produce it.

But, take heart. Prototypes don't have to be expensive, and you don't have to have years of experience to create a venture around an innovative idea. Here are two 16-year-old entrepreneurs who are managing just fine.

PRO FILE

Entrepreneurs: Neeraj Seth and Khurum Ullah
Enterprise: Time Matrix

Neeraj Seth was having problems keeping his high school work organized. He never seemed to have enough time to get things done, and it was affecting his grades. "I realized I needed to be more organized and I thought a better time planner might help," he recalls.

After all, adults use planners all the time, especially in business, so why not high school students? Of course, planners were already available, but the good-quality ones were too expensive for a teenager's budget. Neeraj decided to look into developing a better planner, at a better price, just for students.

He planned to design it on his computer and then get a printing company to run off copies, but he soon realized that he needed a better printer. After pitching the idea to some friends, he took on one of them, Khurum Ullah, who had a better printer, as a partner.

They decided to call their company Time Matrix and began some informal research in the hallways at school. Satisfied that better time management was a broad-based need among their friends, the young entrepreneurs began to set up their new business. They prepared a venture plan in order to get a $3,000 startup loan to get their venture off the ground.

The partners knew their product would have to be innovative, but that didn't seem hard to accomplish. Other planners were essentially just calendars. But Neeraj and Khurum knew they could do better than that. Their planner would be custom-designed for each school, and include special events days, along with the school's rules and regulations, a section on how to study for exams, and a map of the school for newcomers. The finishing touch would be a custom-designed cover with the school's name on it.

A local company was ready to take on the job of printing the planner, but wanted to see a firm order before the presses would roll.

The partners whipped up a letterhead, some design specifications, and a letter of introduction. After phoning and faxing ahead, they took their promotion package to a neighboring high school to pitch their product to the principal. He was impressed, but skeptical. Could these teenagers really deliver? What about a prototype?

And what about the price? Neeraj and his partner decided to sell the planners to high schools at near cost, and then sell advertising space in the back of the planner for profit. This way, they could undercut existing planners by a considerable margin. Advertisers were interested, but they wanted to see a firm order—and a prototype—before they'd commit.

With a self-taught background in computers, they took on the challenging task of working up a prototype. Since they were full-time students as well as entrepreneurs, time planning took on an even more important meaning. The night before their final pitch to their first customer, they finished the prototype.

The next day, the two tired but enthusiastic entrepreneurs closed their first deal. The printer would print and the advertisers would buy. Time Matrix was in business. Sales to date are $5,000. The total startup cost was less than $300 plus a lot of work. Now, they hope to sell their own school on the idea.

 Entrepreneurs need prototypes to prove their venture is viable

The partners at Time Matrix planned carefully and built their team around each other's skills and resources. They also knew the importance of a prototype. Don't be intimidated by the fact that they're teenagers who are running a successful part-time venture. They learned how to be entrepreneurs by doing just what you're doing in this book.

Raising the Money You Need

No matter how modest your idea is, it's going to cost money to get started. Where will you get that money? If you think you might borrow it from a bank or similar lending institution, think again. Unless you have a proven track record in business, a detailed and carefully prepared plan, significant collateral—such as a house, stocks, or bonds—and some of your own money in an account, you're not likely to get very far with your banker. In other words, banks will usually loan you the money if you don't really need it.

In Chapter 2, while practicing communications skills, you tried to see yourself from your banker's perspective. Banks aren't in the business of financing high-risk ventures. You may plan to make a bundle, but the most the bank can earn on your venture is the same rate of interest they earn from a car loan. If a car loan goes bad, at least the bank is left with a used car. If your loan goes bad, they are left with red ink. Furthermore, banks have to answer to their depositors (people who have money in savings accounts) and shareholders (people who own stock in the bank), who don't look favorably on having their money used to finance high-risk schemes. That said, there's a good chance you may still get your financing from a bank. Of course, there's a catch.

Go to the bank

As a first-time entrepreneur, the statistics on success rates for new enterprises aren't on your side. From an objective point of view, you're not a good risk for investment. I have cautioned you not to risk too much on your first go, and you're going to improve your odds a great deal by following the advice in this book, but you could still end up with an excellent learning experience and no money. At least, that's how your banker will probably think of you and your prospects. The easiest way to get your bank to loan you money for your venture is to have someone else shoulder the risk. You may need someone who will co-sign or guarantee your loan, who will risk his or her collateral, good name, and reputation on you.

If you're like most first-time entrepreneurs, that person is your close friend or a family member—someone who knows and believes in you. Many people think it's bad policy to loan money to a family member, and many others are embarrassed to approach their family for money. But, in most cases, just as with first-time mortgage money, that's where first-time entrepreneurs get their startup cash.

Most likely, it will be your mother, father, mother-in-law, father-in-law, sister, brother, aunt, uncle, or best friend—or any combination of those people—who will take a chance on you and your idea. Assuming one or more of them can either guarantee a bank loan or loan you the money directly, what do you think it will take to convince them to do that?

Do they trust you?

A lot will depend on your track record with them. If you've tapped your friends and relatives for money before and not paid them back promptly, or at all, you shouldn't be surprised if they don't look up from re-runs of "Leave it to Beaver" when you make your pitch for another loan. But, you know how things stand with them, and you'll know whether you have a chance or not. No matter how much they like and respect you, it's not likely they're going to write you a blank check. After all, one of the reasons they might have money to loan in the first place is because they haven't frittered it away on hare-brained schemes in the past. You'll have to convince them yours isn't such a hare-brained scheme.

In short, you'll have to tell them exactly how you intend to make your venture pay, so that you can repay them—or the banker who's holding their collateral. What questions do you think you'd have to answer to get their support? Try this exercise to find out. It's a pretend funding-pitch session with your relatives and friends.

EXERCISE 23

Task: To answer your relatives' and friends' questions about your entrepreneurial venture

Objective: To convince them to loan you startup money

Imagine that your potential investors are gathered to hear your pitch. Fill in your answers to the following commonly asked questions. Each question has an evaluation (what they hope to hear as an answer).

1. Q: So, what's all this about? Why do you want to do this?

    A: _____

       _____

       _____

       _____

Evaluation

Your motivation is important.

Whether they're family or friends, your potential investors are really considering investing in you, more than your idea. They know it will take persistence to see your venture through, and they want to be convinced that you really are committed. So, your job is to convince them that this venture is something you really believe in, that it complements and fits your abilities, and that you're interested in it, regardless of how rich it might make you.

For example, let's say you're planning to open a clothing store for big and tall people. If you're big, tall, or both, if you know who fits this description and how difficult it is to find clothes that fit and flatter, and if you've always wanted to be in the retail clothing business and you have some experience as a salesperson, you have a number of excellent reasons to want to pursue your venture.

2. Q: What are you selling?

    A: _____

        _____

        _____

        _____

Evaluation

This sounds easy, but it can be a trick question. It's crucially important that you understand the real reason people would loan money for your venture.

You should be able to demonstrate a thorough understanding of your product or service, and the need it addresses. Are you selling memberships in a fitness club or are you selling health? Also, you should be clear about sizes, colors, suppliers, quantities, and any other details about your product, such as who would be offering the service, business hours, location, and types of employees.

Consider the example of the big and tall clothing store. People need clothing, to be sure, but is that the real need you're satisfying? You might think you're just selling specialty clothing—but you might well be selling convenience, self-confidence, and understanding. This will make a difference in how you service your customers.

3. Q: Who are your customers?

    A: _____

        _____

        _____

        _____

Evaluation

As much as possible, you should know the age, sex, income bracket, and purchasing habits of your customers—in short, everything you could find out through formal or informal research.

Of course, you know that customers for your big and tall shop will be big or tall, or both. But are they male or female or both? Affluent? Middle class? Age 15 to 25? 25 to 45? 45 to 65? You'll need to know, so you can offer the right kind of service and product.

4. Q: What makes your idea so special?

    A: _____

        _____

        _____

        _____

Evaluation

You have to be clear about why anyone would need what you intend to offer, and why they'd choose you and your product or service over someone else's.

To stand out from your competition, you have to have the first such venture, or the best product, or the best price, or the most quantity, or any combination thereof. Or your venture has to be innovative in some other way.

In the big and tall shop example, you might offer upscale clothing where others don't, or you might offer hats and accessories where others don't. Or you might hire only big and tall staff, who would be more in tune with your clientele.

5. Q: Who will you get to help you with this?

A: _____

_____

_____

_____

Evaluation

You should know you can't do everything yourself. Your potential investors want to be reassured that they'll get their money back someday; they don't necessarily care how many people you have to share your profits with. They want to know you'll get the best possible people for the job and that you know where you can find them.

6. Q: When are you planning to start up and what will you do first?

A: _____

_____

_____

_____

Evaluation

You should be making the case that the only thing missing from your plans is startup capital. So, if you have them hooked, and it looks like you're going to get your money, you'd better be able to say what you're going to do with it, and when.

Whether it's signing the lease on your building, hiring staff, or scouting a location, you should be able to justify the sequence of each of the steps you're about to take.

7. Q: Let's say it works. Then what?

A: _____

_____

_____

▶ ▶ ▶ ▶▶▶▶▶

Evaluation

You won't start at the top; you'll have to work your way there. But you want to have some idea of what you'd do if you're successful. Will you franchise? Expand? Sell? Choose the best option, the one that suits your resources and aspirations. But make sure you know what you're talking about.

8. Q: When do you think you'd be able to pay me back?

A: _____

_____

_____

_____

Evaluation

This is the kicker. You're not asking for a gift, you're asking for a loan, and loans have to be repaid. Your potential investors know there's risk here, or you wouldn't be needing their money—you could just get it from a bank. They understand that it's difficult to predict how a new venture will perform, especially when it's being shepherded by a novice entrepreneur. But you should have done your homework and figured out, as closely as possible, what kind of sales and cash flow you expect to generate over the next year or two. And you should attach a repayment plan to those estimates.

9. Q: What are you going to do if this whole thing blows up in your face?

A: _____

_____

_____

_____

Evaluation

First you have to know that it can happen, and secondly you have to know what it would be like if it did happen. Play that scenario over in your mind and ask yourself, "Can I survive this? Am I prepared to risk that possibility?" If you aren't prepared to survive the worst-case scenario, you should look for a safer venture. Nobody wants to see you destroyed, and nobody wants to see that you have no backup plans. Also, Uncle Vito and Aunt Mary don't want to lose their money either. You should make sure you have something to fall back on before you start.

10. Q: You're going to leave your nice, secure job for this?

A: _____

_____

_____

_____

_____

Evaluation

Everyone wants to make sure you're going into this with your eyes open. Every opportunity costs something. If you choose the steak from the menu, you have to give up the fish. Convince your potential investors that you know what you're giving up and that you won't change your mind in a week or two. For example, if you're now working as a clerk at a clothing store, earning minimum wage, your jump to the big and tall shop will be more reasonable and understandable. But, if you're leaving a position with a high salary and a generous pension plan, you'll need to be more convincing.

11.Q: Are you sure you know how much you need to get started?

A: _____

_____

_____

_____

Evaluation

Too often new enterprises go under because the entrepreneur underestimated how much startup money would be needed. If you don't have accounting experience, show that you've sought sound financial advice. Either way, make sure you can demonstrate that you've carefully costed the whole process. Then build some backup capital into your plans, just to be safe. You'll likely need it.

 The venture plan is the entrepreneur's road map to success

Congratulations! You've just completed your homework for a basic venture plan! If you were able to answer those 11 questions satisfactorily, you are more prepared than many entrepreneurs when they start up. Of course, you should write all the information down in a nice, neat format (see the sample venture plan on page 197) so that you can make copies for your investors. They will likely want tangible proof of your research and written evidence of your intentions. A promissory note (I.O.U.) wouldn't be out of the question, either.

What's that you say? You don't need to borrow?

What if you have to convince only yourself that you have a good idea? You already have the money saved up and you're ready to roll. Since you're willing to risk your own money, it's likely that the people you hire to help you will hitch a ride on your confidence (you'll still need a team because you won't be able to do everything yourself). So, they'll probably nod and smile and make you feel even more confident (if the money runs out, it's likely they will, too).

In this case, you'll have to be particularly cautious. If you don't have a relatively disinterested third party examining your venture, you're probably getting a very biased assessment of your chances of success. As odd as it may sound, the best thing you could do would be to find a qualified, neutral third party to try to convince you why you shouldn't undertake your venture. A trusted accountant or financial adviser would fill that bill. (See Chapter 6 for tips on how to select an outside adviser, if you don't already have one.)

Remember that car you just couldn't wait to buy?

It's hard, and sometimes offputting, to temper your enthusiasm deliberately with some negative input. But at times like these, you'd do well to remember other deals you might have cut prematurely. Remember that cherry-red, zillion-horsepower dream machine that you just had to have—right now? (Or that living room ensemble, boat, set of encyclopedias, tattoo, or the bald look you went for one crazy day?) Remember how, after a couple of days, you discovered the rust under the wheel wells and the pool of oil on the driveway? Remember that sick feeling? The term for that feeling is buyers' remorse. It's the feeling you get when you have serious second thoughts about your purchase—after the fact.

You don't want to find out that your sure thing isn't so sure after you've quit your job and committed your savings to it.

Take a cold shower

In many ways it would be better if you had to borrow the money to get started. That way you'd have to convince someone else that your scheme has merit. That way, you'd be forced to plan. If you really do intend to risk your own money, protect your interests. Cool off a bit and see if your idea can survive some objective scrutiny—from critics whose perspectives are different from yours.

Get some input

No doubt you've noticed that our world is blessed with all kinds of people. For instance, you probably know some of them:

- The pessimists look for the funeral when they smell flowers.
- The fact freaks test the quality of a joke by counting how many seconds people laugh at it.
- The intuitive types say, "I just know this horse will win the race."
- The practical types say, "What do I have to do and when do I have to do it?"
- The optimists say, "No problem. I just finished tossing a bottle with a note into the water, so we'll be off this island in no time."
- The creative types say, "Think of all the possibilities! Why, you could do this and that at the same time, and..."

A good way to assess your venture is to have representatives of each personality type evaluate your idea. You may disagree with each of their perspectives, but, if you're going to succeed, you'll need to be a little of each. If you can't get a group like this together to examine your idea, try to put yourself in their shoes and do it yourself. Just ask yourself, "How would a pessimist view my plans, and why?" Work through the spectrum of perspectives and see what happens.

EXERCISE 24

Task: To evaluate your venture from different points of view
Objective: To make sure you've covered all bases

Do this exercise if possible with people who really do represent these types—even one or two would be a help. Ask each one their reactions to your scheme, what questions they might ask, and how you might answer them. If you have only one person to play with you, share the role-playing tasks. The examples will help keep you on track. Use a separate sheet of paper.

> Pessimist ("What if you get sick?")
> Intuitive person ("What's your gut feeling about this?")
> Practical type ("How are you planning to handle your cash?")
> Optimist ("What are you going to do when you get rich?")
> Creative type ("Have you considered these other possibilities?")

Evaluation
Even if you didn't like some of the questions, were you able to provide answers that satisfied you? Did you raise any new doubts that you couldn't resolve? Which perspective is most like yours? You may not be an optimist. You may be very practical. If so, you may need some creative input, or you might work harder than necessary for less money than you could get. Try to imagine these types hovering around as you get started.

And remember—you need feedback. You want feedback. It's your best hedge against potential problems.

 Entrepreneurs need feedback

Prying Open the Window of Opportunity

Most entrepreneurs in search of opportunity look around for a need that nobody else is filling. But some—not satisfied to be shut out of a field that really interests them, just because somebody else has tried it—use research and planning like a scalpel to carefully carve out a niche. It's not for the faint of heart, but Dan Sitnam has proven that it can be done.

Entrepreneur: Dan Sitnam

Enterprise: Helijet Airways, Inc.

Everybody said it would never fly. Others had considered operating a passenger helicopter service between Vancouver, on the mainland of British Columbia, Canada, and that province's capital city, Victoria, less than 160 km (100 miles) away on Vancouver Island. But Dan Sitnam loves a challenge and thought it could be done. No one had succeeded, for various reasons.

From the outset, Dan knew he'd have to do everything right. There was no margin for error. But the opportunity seemed obvious. There were only three ways to travel between British Columbia's two largest cities: by ferry, which takes several hours; by commercial airliner, which requires travelling to airports, both of them some distance outside the cities; and by pontoon-equipped aircraft, which can't fly when the weather is foggy or rainy—and that's often in that part of the world.

As an experienced helicopter pilot, Dan knew that helicopters could make the trip from downtown to downtown as fast as, or faster than, float planes and in most types of weather. He knew that helicopter pilots would welcome the opportunity to work near their homes, rather than in the remote locations where they usually found work. He also knew that there were reasons others had failed in their attempts to provide the service.

First he studied those failures. He discovered that people consid-

ered helicopters noisy and not suitable as passenger vehicles, and that the previous operators had chosen the wrong type of helicopter and had operated with the strategy of charter rather than regular service. Dan figured that if he could overcome these problems, he could make his new company viable.

He managed to raise enough capital to test the market. He chose a quiet 12-passenger helicopter and began to offer introductory rates to potential customers. They liked it. But the communities he flew over didn't care for the noise, so Dan began a round of community meetings, where he listened to the complaints and offered alternatives. He decided to fly higher than helicopters normally flew and avoid flying directly over communities, where possible. The complaints stopped.

Helijet Airways was launched with one helicopter and a staff of 15 employees. Airlines traditionally operate with very slim profit margins and, with Dan's overhead, it was clear that profits would be slim, indeed. To reduce costs, Dan made special arrangements with the helicopter engine manufacturers so that his own company could perform light overhauls. Instead of initially purchasing expensive airline reservation software, he found a way to use hotel-reservation software, at considerable savings.

It wasn't easy. Financially, the company barely managed to stay aloft. But his attention to detail and

> efficiency of operation started to pay off. Eight years after he started up, Dan's company now operates six helicopters and business is booming. He gives his employees much of the credit for Helijet's success.
>
> "I see us as a team. The people at Helijet came aboard looking for a challenge. I have 100 overachievers here and I see my job as feeding the fire, so to speak."

If Dan Sitnam had overlooked any of hundreds of details, Helijet would have gone the way of other passenger helicopter services. But his planning was scrupulous. He worked away at every conceivable factor that would affect the viability of his venture, and he succeeded in securing a niche in the airline industry. Not everyone can set up a new airline, but your success or failure in exploiting a niche market will probably be determined by how carefully you take care of the little details of your venture.

 Niche markets reward entrepreneurs who plan scrupulously

Planning: A final word

When you pitch your plan to potential investors, one of the key ingredients they'll be looking for is your "team fit"—team members who will complement and mesh with each other's abilities and interests. Your investors will want to know who's going to be doing all the tasks that you aren't capable of, or won't have time for. Next to raising the money to get started, choosing the team that will help build your venture is the most important task you'll have.

There is a certain amount of "which-comes-first-the-chicken-or-the-egg" to this process, however. You may have trouble raising the money if you can't demonstrate that you'll have a good team fit, and you can't promise to hire people until you have the money to get started. You'll have to approach potential team players in advance, secure their interest, and then return later with a concrete offer.

Team Building

Dan Sitnam is like most successful entrepreneurs when he describes his role as "feeding the fire." He took a great deal of care in choosing his team and the roles they would play in his venture, and now he sees his main task as keeping them challenged. How are you picking your team and how do you see your role relative to theirs?

You learned a bit about the importance of teamwork in Chapter 2. Now that you're starting up, you'll have to pay particular attention to building your team, motivating your team, and letting your team work.

You like your friends and you love your family, but you don't have to like or love the people who'll help you get your venture up and running. Down the road a few years, you may be able to fine-tune your team to include people you genuinely like, who also happen to be the best people for the job. For now, you should concentrate on getting people who know what they're doing and who are motivated to do it.

You can't afford not to care how they work with the other members of your team. They'll be working with each other a lot more than they'll be working with you. You may want to see yourself as one of the gang, but you're probably kidding yourself. You hired them. They work for you and you're the boss. That relationship tends to be set. But, how team members relate to each other is critically important, and you can have a great deal of influence on how well they work together.

First, there was just you, then...?

Whom should you hire first? Since the most common pitfalls entrepreneurs encounter involve financial management, it seems appropriate that you hire an accountant or financial adviser first. You'll be making financial decisions from the start, so you'll need someone to hold your hand. Depending on your needs, you might hire someone part-time, or as needed. (See Chapter 6 for suggestions on how to evaluate and decide whose advice to seek.) But be aware that the role of the accountant is changing. These days, many accountants act as senior financial advisers to their firms. Rather than being just bean-counters, they're part of every major decision some companies make.

You're hiring a whole person

After you have secured a reputable financial adviser, the next person you should hire depends largely on what type of venture you're building. But you can head off some potential problems by being careful not to take too narrow a view of your candidates' roles and abilities. Just because you hired an injection-mold specialist doesn't mean you should restrict that person to that role. That same person might also be an excellent team leader, problem solver or settler of disputes. In one case, an media entrepreneur hired a receptionist who showed an interest in becoming a producer. Within a year, that receptionist had become the top-grossing producer on staff. Make sure you allow and encourage your team members to expand their roles, if they're capable.

Build a competent, empowered team

You have to hire people for their skills, not because of their connections to you. That way each member will feel proud to be working in such a skilled group and not be dragged down by some relative, who clearly was hired only because he needs work or because his dad or mom financed your venture.

As you build the team, keep personalities in mind. Avoid putting two confrontational people on the same team, for example. Where possible, let existing team members help select new members. They'll tend to take more responsibility for their selection and they'll also feel that their decisions are respected and valuable. They'll feel more empowered.

Money is a prime motivator—people won't want to work for less than they feel they're worth—but empowerment can make up for some financial shortcomings. Promises of "riches down the road" won't wash with most people. They've likely heard that before. But if you can't pay the going rate, you can earn loyalty by sharing profits or selling shares in your venture to key people. If your team members own a piece of the action, they're more likely to go the extra distance to get the job done. Even a small percentage can make a big difference. When your venture takes off, everyone on your team will feel they're taking off with it. Equity (or ownership) is a great motivator.

Sometimes building a team is less formal and does involve friends. But in these cases, the friends often become partners, not employees. Sometimes, as in the following profile, their involvement can make the difference between a venture's having a life, or wasting away on a shelf.

PRO FILE

Entrepreneur: John Kozen

Enterprise: Concept Food Group

John Kozen grew up around restaurants so he knew a thing or two about food. When he completed his education he branched out into restaurant design, while his father, Gerry, continued to explore new food possibilities in the restaurant business. Using his technical expertise, Gerry was working on a way of mass-producing a new kind of cheese stick—something like a fish stick, but smaller and made with cheese—when he ran into marketing problems and decided to shelve the idea for the time being.

Years passed. A recession arrived and John found he had more office space than he could use. His friend, Jeff, who had good contacts in the supermarket chains, needed some more space, so Jeff moved in. John had some time on his hands, so he resurrected the cheese stick idea and ran it past Jeff, who loved it, and agreed to be John and Gerry's partner on the venture.

They brought the product up to standard, made some samples and pitched the product to a supermarket chain. On this attempt, the timing

▶ ▶ ▶ ▶▶▶▶▶

was right. The supermarket was looking for hors d'oeuvres for the coming holiday season and wanted to include the new product in their print promotion. The cheese sticks were a big hit, and now John, Jeff, and Gerry are working on new versions of their product to meet the growing demand.

It took a few years for Gerry's technical expertise to mesh with Jeff's contacts and John's time, but when the time was right, the entrepreneurs were ready.

John and Jeff's venture is a good example of how important it is to hold off on starting up until the right team is in place.

You're supposed to steer, not interfere

You're the captain of the ship. You decide where it's going and why it's going there. Your job is to encourage and help your team members do their jobs as well as possible so your venture will stay on schedule. But don't confuse helping with interfering. Your people will let you know when and how you can help. Listen to them. They want the freedom and responsibility to do their jobs, and they want to know that you support them in that mission.

Your main job, as entrepreneur, is to chart the course and avoid disaster. Too often the boss assumes that everyone else either doesn't really care where the venture is going, or that it's obvious and everyone automatically knows. As always, assumptions are dangerous.

Meetings, necessary meetings

Even though you're just getting started, you won't likely be working alone. Whether you're working with one partner or a larger team, you need to communicate well, right from the start. You'll recall some tips on communicating with your employees from Chapter 2. Here's another look:

- Schedule regular meetings. The more often you meet, the shorter these meetings will become. Tell everyone what you're currently working on and why. Update and explain the general progress of the venture. Have each of your teams report on their works-in-progress. Listen to complaints and comments. Afterward, prepare a brief summary of the meeting and give a copy to each employee.

- Schedule regular team meetings. These will be more task-specific and your role in them will be more that of a listener and supporter.

- When you run into trouble, let everyone know right away. They won't be impressed if they hear about problems through the grapevine before they hear about them from you. They'll appreciate your honesty and they may well be able to offer solutions.

- If you're in an office, and you like to have your own private space, follow an open-door policy. Unless you're with a client, or taking an important call, leave your door open and encourage your colleagues and employees to walk in whenever they feel the need. Make the time.
- If this is the first time you've ever wielded power, be careful you aren't seduced by it. It can be very tempting to turn your office into a throne room, where you can hold court and pontificate. If you're so tempted, remember how little you appreciated being dictated to by former employers. Your people will feel the same way.

You're one of a kind, but so is everyone else

Whether you use power to drive your team singlemindedly toward your goals, or, less admirably, you begin to enjoy a power trip, beware. You've probably heard the saying "Power corrupts." It's often used to explain patronage and graft. But power can corrupt in other ways. For example, once you're in power, you might start believing that you aren't like these people. After a while, you may give up trying to explain your vision and direction as a waste of time. Before you know it, you've become an elitist.

If this sounds like you, you're making a big mistake. By now, you should have learned from this book that everyone has a dream—it's just that everyone doesn't have your dream. Your employees are more like you than they're different. If you want proof of that, alienate them to the point where they jump ship and start their own operation—in competition with you! It happens more often than you'd like to think. "Gee," you think, after the fact, "I didn't think she had it in her." If you're going to assume anything, assume that all your employees are entrepreneurs in varying stages of development. They're on their way somewhere and they're willing to merge their dream with yours for as long as you can sustain their interest. That means respecting their abilities and aspirations—and their need to know what's going on.

People like to know why they're doing something. Like you, they're really not just in it for the money. At least, money won't keep them motivated for long. They want to see the big picture—how they and their work fit in. It's your job to describe that big picture and to make sure it's a clear and attractive one.

You're just getting started. As you bring others into your venture, you should make sure you get off on the right foot. You'll have plenty of daily challenges to overcome without adding interpersonal problems to your load.

A day without problems is not likely

Day-to-day entrepreneurship seems to be more about defining and solving problems than anything else. At any given time, everybody has at least one problem in varying stages of being solved or being discovered. Some people actually like problems; they thrive on finding solutions.

Teamwork is one good way to solve problems. Turn your teams loose on a problem and stand back. Encourage them to be creative, go crazy, try new ways of doing things. If they fail—after trying hard—praise them for showing you a clear way not to solve the problem. If they succeed, give them all the credit—after all, you had the good sense to put the team together, so you can pat yourself on the back, in private, later.

Let your team define the problem themselves. Too often solutions evade problem solvers because they're working on the wrong problem. Remember the convenience store parking lot problem in Chapter 3, where different employees defined a problem in different ways and some even saw it as an opportunity. The latter is not only more common than you'd think, it also hints at the reason you shouldn't fear problems, but rather, see them as a minefield of opportunities.

Partners: Can't live with 'em, can't live without 'em

Profit or not-for-profit, your venture won't likely go far without partners to share the risks and work.

You'll probably be in partnership with somebody in the course of your venture, and that can be a very good thing. Partnerships reduce risk by pooling resources and skills, no argument about that. Generally, partners take profits out according to the risk they've taken getting in, and according to what they've put in since startup. There are often arguments about that.

Partnerships often start out: "With my brains and your money, we'll be rich in no time!" They often end up: "Seems to me I'm doing all the work, while you're getting all the money!"

As in personal relationships, too often people look for partners who are just like themselves. It's almost a warning sign when someone says, "It's amazing! We both like the same things: the same food, the same music, and the same fashions!" A certain amount of similarity is essential, but what if you both hate to do the same things? Who'll do them?

There's a saying about a farmer who says, speaking of her husband, "We're a perfect match. I like horses and he doesn't." Look for a partner who complements your abilities and interests. That way you won't bump into each other as much, and you won't resent the other person for getting to do all the good stuff. If you like meeting new people, you might be better suited to marketing than your partner, who, preferring to work at a desk, might be better suited to office administration.

You wouldn't choose a partner you couldn't trust. But, even if one partner doesn't deliberately try to work less and grab more than a fair share, there can be problems. Verbal arrangements such as, "You'll be busy with your family on weekends and I understand," often prove worthless, especially if one partner is prone to workaholic tendencies or doesn't have a family.

The best way to keep things on an even keel is to have a formal written, partnership agreement. Lawyers can help here. Better to have a lawyer help you set up the partnership agreement than to deal later with the legal consequences of not having your terms on paper. These agreements don't have to be lengthy or complicated. They simply spell out what each expects of the other and include a good "what if" clause. Yes, just as in romantic relationships, people can change and become vindictive. Even the best partnerships sometimes sour, and it's best to think about this possibility before the fact.

In case of dispute, get the shotgun!
A shotgun agreement seems to work very well in cases of a simple partnership between two people. Here's how it works: The partners agree that, at any time, one partner can offer to buy the other partner out. This is called "loading the shotgun." The other partner now has the option either to accept the offer or to buy the initiator out for the same price. That's called "pulling the trigger." The beauty of this arrangement is that the price is guaranteed to be right.

If you know that your offer can be turned back on you, you'll be very sure to make it fair. If you think your partner has greatly underestimated the value of the business, reflected in the offer to you, you can take advantage of what you perceive to be a good deal and buy him or her out.

In theory, this agreement can work for three partners, but it gets a little complex. You might want to bring lawyers in at that point.

Like marriage, partnership is a two-way street
In some ways, partners are closer than married couples. You may see your husband or wife for only a couple of hours a day, but you might be with your partner for 14 hours straight. The best advice is to be mature, empathize, accommodate, and apologize. Don't ask what for, you'll have plenty of occasions. Nothing replaces good old "please" and "thank you," and nothing sours a relationship faster than taking someone for granted. Finally, don't let tensions build in silence. Talk to each other.

 Entrepreneurs nurture and value partnerships

The Profit Motive

Your partnerships are sealed, your team is built, and all is in place. You've done your planning and are confident all is shipshape. All that's left to do is make money.

Ultimately, the main reason for careful planning is to ensure that your venture will make money. Sometimes, in spite of a well-prepared venture plan, the fundamentals of turning a profit are lost along the way. It's amazing how many businesses appear to be rolling along—teams working, problems being solved, paper flying, computer terminals glowing, and printers and fax machines humming—but aren't making any money! We're not talking rocket science here; this is dead easy. It's so simple, one wonders how so many can get it wrong. You buy something or provide a service. You sell it for more than you paid for it or you charge for your services. What's left over is called profit. Profit is what you pay yourself so you can buy groceries and, perhaps, expand the business.

You wouldn't last long in business if you were buying boxes of soap for $2 and selling them for $1.50, would you? Well, that's the equivalent of what some entrepreneurs are actually doing. When they add up all their overhead costs (salaries, rent, equipment, telephone, and so on) and then add up all their sales, they find there's nothing left. If they raise their prices to try to improve the situation, their customers run to the competition, which has lower overhead, for some reason.

In over your head!

In this case, it's pretty clear that overhead has to be cut, but how? Whom do you fire? What do you cut? How can you be more productive? Often the difference between profit and loss is the sum of dozens of small costs that add to your cost of sales. Imagine you're showing a loss of $5,000 for a month in which you had $50,000 in sales. Changing your suppliers, buying in bulk, or offering to pay on delivery rather than in 30 days, might save you 10% on your stationery and packaging. Now, find a way to save 10% on your telephone bills, rent, staffing, and electricity. In other words, reduce your cost of sales by 10%, and you're out of the red and into the black!

If you know your cost of sales, and you've tightened up all the details of your operation, you'll have a secure basis on which to change or build your venture. If you're still not making money, you at least know where you don't have problems, and can address larger, more structural changes armed with that knowledge.

Profit isn't a luxury. It's a necessity. Of course, when you're starting up you'll have to do some work "on spec" (short for speculation, which means you work hard, at your own expense, trying to land a contract in the hopes that it will pay off later). That work will be absorbed into your overall profit and loss. But, the best advice is to try to establish a positive cash flow as soon as possible. That means: have something to sell for cash on day one and keep it that way.

KEY POINT Profit, to an entrepreneur, is what others call wages

There is one exception to this rule, but it has a catch...

No profit? No loss...necessarily

It will likely take money to do any type of venture, but not all ventures aim to make piles of money. For example, you may be interested in setting up a food bank to help the hungry and desperate people in your community. You hope to get people to donate food to a central depot, where it will be distributed among the needy. Your profit won't be money; it will be fewer hungry people. In fact, the fewer people who need your bank, the more profitable you'll be. But make no mistake; yours is still a venture in every sense of the word, and, as such, it can benefit from the same type of planning.

Now that you've had a chance to learn about the entrepreneurial process, here's a visual summary of that process:

The Entrepreneur's Environment

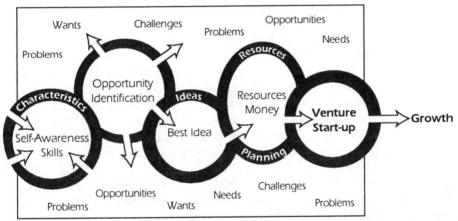

In Chapter 6 you'll see how to use strategic planning to manage growth. Before you turn the page, here's a summary of the key points in Chapter 5.

 Summary

> It's important to plan, but it's more important to take that
>   first step
> Nobody does it exactly right the first time or every time
> Entrepreneurs need prototypes to prove their venture is viable
> The plan is the entrepreneur's road map to success
> Entrepreneurs need feedback
> Niche markets reward entrepreneurs who plan scrupulously
> Entrepreneurs nurture and value partnerships
> Profit, to an entrepreneur, is what others call wages

6 Managing Growth

"Standing still is going backwards."

    ⁊ TOM DROOG,
      ENTREPRENEUR

Whether you have a venture under way or you're just exploring the possibility, you need to understand that enterprises, like children, grow. And, like children, if they're not growing, they might be ill. Growth is usually a good thing. Properly managed, it will allow you to make more profits. But it can also be necessary for survival. If you're offering an innovative product or service, lots of people are going to want it, and, if you're not big enough to serve them all, a competitor will come along and do it for you. But unplanned growth or growth for its own sake may not be good at all. You need to know why you're growing and you need to control that growth—you can't let growth control you. In this chapter, you'll:

• learn why it's important to control and manage growth
• get some tips on how to anticipate and deal with potential problems
• meet someone who specializes in finding advice for entrepreneurs
• have a chance to practice some strategic planning
• learn some of the language that strategic planners use
• learn how to survive a recession
• deal with the manager-versus-entrepreneur dilemma.

Don't Stand Still

It's impossible to know exactly how many customers or clients you're going to have in the future, but you can do a great deal to predict and manage the growth of your venture. One of the reasons that you're attracted to entrepreneurship is that you like to be in control of your destiny. It's one thing to control your venture's creation and startup, but you're going to have to refine certain skills such as management, problem solving, and decision making to be able to control its expansion. It's all about being in control.

Who's driving?

If you're a driver, do you remember your first car? It probably wasn't much to look at, and it likely couldn't win any races, but you probably thought it was just great. Not only did it represent freedom, it also got you where you wanted to go. It gave you control!

By the time it made its last trip, dangling on the end of a tow truck, you knew that car inside out. Not only could you drive it when no one else could, you also knew all its little noises and rattles, and the problems they foretold. And you may have even known how to head off major repairs with preventive maintenance. ("Pull over, the radiator's going to blow!")

Your first venture will be very much like your first car, and the same principles apply. It may rattle and shake, it may start off slowly, and it may take constant personal maintenance, but it will get you where you want to go. Just like that old car, the faster your venture goes, the better your driving skills have to be to control it safely. And just as you learned to manage your car, within its limitations, and got it to take you more places to do more things, you'll learn how to manage your venture and get it to accomplish more and more. That's because, as an entrepreneur, you're interested in nurturing a venture, not just creating a one-person job.

To control or be controlled

Even if you don't want to grow, you may not have a choice about the matter. What if you open a sandwich shop and it turns out that people are just crazy about your sandwiches and service? One of your customers might offer you a contract to supply a whole construction site at a time when you're barely able to keep up with the lunch-hour demand. What do you do? If, like most first-time entrepreneurs, you've worked long, hard hours just to get started, you may be tempted to jump at any deal you're offered, especially if it's a big one. "Don't!" says Tom Droog.

PRO FILE

Entrepreneur: Tom Droog

Enterprise: Alberta Sunflower Seeds Ltd.

Tom Droog always wanted to be a farmer, but land is scarce in the Netherlands, where he was born and raised. As soon as he was able, Tom headed to North America. "I went to the West," he says, "because I wanted to go where they grow sugar beets and potatoes." Tom had saved enough money to buy a small farm, where he grew sugar beets, wheat, and flax, but he decided that he wanted to grow produce that he could market himself rather than through a government agency. "I wanted more

145

marketing options," says Tom. "That's why I decided to grow sunflower seeds. You can use them for oil, feed, or human consumption."

Tom tried producing different sunflower seed products and soon settled on the snack market. He cleaned, roasted, salted, and bagged the seeds, which he called Spitz. "People who like to eat sunflower seeds right out of the shell often call them 'spits,'" Tom explains. In order to make an impression on the existing market and build new markets, Tom knew he had to be innovative. "We tried things that were completely different. We came out with three flavors of seeds, and we used a resealable bag."

When Tom Droog took on the birdseed market, his business began to grow quickly. Soon he was encouraging other farmers to grow sunflowers so he could buy their crops to augment his own. "Sometimes I wish you could just make growth stand still," sighs Tom. "But you can't, because standing still is going backwards."

"My key job is controlling growth," Tom continues. "I control selling, quality, and construction of new facilities. It's easier to build than to rebuild. When I build, I make a point of building big, and it's a good thing, because our growth has been phenomenal. A few years ago we were filling 50,000 bags of Spitz per year. Now we're filling 95,000 per day! Another thing—I finance all my growth out of cash flow. I do that by building a little bit each year, as I can afford it."

Tom is careful to deliver the same high quality to his customers, no matter how big his company grows. "I control quality," Tom repeats. "You take birdseed, for instance. Birds don't know if the seeds have been cleaned (the weeds and trash removed) or not. But birds aren't buying the seeds—people are. And people want to be sure the quality is there. So we clean them—perfectly!"

"When you grow the way our company has grown, you have to look at the market differently," Tom says. "Although I'm servicing an existing market, I'm also creating a market where one had not existed, because I'm getting more and more people to try our products."

In peak season, Tom employs 32 people in various stages of his operation. A further 35 work as freelance distributors, and Tom keeps a close eye on their work as well. "I know how well a certain territory should be doing," Tom explains, "and if I see that sales aren't what they should be, I take action. In one case recently, I changed distributors and saw sales rise by 30%."

Each year Tom convenes his employees to consolidate and stabilize the existing operations. Once he's satisfied that production is keeping pace with sales, he sets out his new plans for growth. They include encouraging his employees and distributors to be creative and try new things. "I'm an entrepreneur," Tom says, "so I have to give my employees room to be entrepreneurial, too. It makes sense."

 Entrepreneurs control the growth of their venture

Tom Droog's success is largely a result of his careful approach to growth. He makes sure he can deliver the quantity and quality of products his customers demand, before he takes on new contracts. It's very important to know your capacity to deliver before you sign a big, new contract.

If you ignore reality, sign the big contract, and can't deliver, you probably won't get a second chance. Even if you can gear up to deliver on that contract, you'd have to be developing more large contracts to make use of your increased capacity, lest you're stuck with it—and the overhead it carries. If you double your contracts overnight, you'll have to double every aspect of your operation: warehousing, production, distribution, and support staff. Even more importantly, if you get bogged down trying to fill the big contract, you might short-change your established customers in the process, and you can't afford to lose a loyal customer.

Lost customers are lost income. If you lose one, you might lose more. Bad news spreads quickly. Customers talk to each other and they might cut you off before you can make trouble for them. But, most importantly, it costs much more time and money to win a new customer than it does to hold on to an established one. You don't have to sell an established customer every time. Established customers know your product lines and your ways of doing business—there are no surprises. Few people are more important to your venture than loyal customers. These people are your most valuable asset. Don't overlook them or stampede over them in a headlong pursuit of growth. Not only will you not get them back, they'll also take others with them.

You've probably seen signs like this in places of business: "If you like our service, tell your friends. If you don't like it, tell us!" Unfortunately, customers usually do the opposite. If they like your service or product, they may not tell anyone, even though they quietly return for more. But if they don't like your service or product, they may quietly leave and then tell everyone they know what a lousy establishment you run. You've probably done that yourself. As much as you like good products and services, you usually don't get worked up about them. But, you really get annoyed when you get lousy service or a poor product.

Quality counts

That's why, as you grow, one of the biggest challenges you'll have to deal with is keeping quality high. If you've ever said, "Since they got so big, they're just not as good as they used to be," you've been a victim of the bigger-is-better philosophy.

Your growth should be good for your customers, not bad. As you get bigger, you should be able to offer more variety, faster service, and maybe even better prices. If you take that route, your customers will cheer you on.

Don't let your valued customers suffer through longer waits at the checkout, abrupt changes in policy ("We don't accept checks any more"), or reduced quality of products.

You can help head off these potential problems by:
- growing slowly and carefully
- informing your clients about changes before you implement them
- properly training new staff and having old staff "shadow" new staff for a while
- making sure your staffing keeps pace with growth
- identifying and rewarding valued customers
- keeping the quality of products and services high.

Customer loyalty: Earn it, buy it, and nurture it

One way to help ensure manageable growth is to hang on to your old customers while you attract new ones. Customer loyalty becomes especially important during economic downturns, when it's valued the most, but it should be front and center, regardless of the state of the economy.

There are a number of marketing schemes designed to create and foster customer loyalty. Car manufacturers are now sponsoring credit cards that allow consumers to rack up a percentage of everyday purchases against the cost of a new car. Once consumers start building credits toward the cost of one manufacturer's vehicles, they may be likely to stay with that one rather than switch to another in midstream.

Among the most popular marketing schemes are the travel points programs. In these programs, participating businesses join with credit card companies and airlines to offer customers redeemable travel points as bonuses for everyday purchases. For example, a consumer who uses a particular credit card to buy any product or service is awarded a certain number of travel points, which can then be used to obtain free tickets on a participating airline. In some cases, no credit card is required. Consumers are invited to join a club, which allows them to collect points for any type of purchase regardless of the method of payment.

Participating businesses report significant increases in customer loyalty. It makes sense. Once customers have built up a significant number of points, they're more motivated to keep shopping at businesses where they can continue to build points. They just keep coming back for more.

But, if you're just a novice entrepreneur with a small business, you won't be able to undertake such grandiose schemes. You'll have to rely on the quality of your service and the personal attention you give your clients to instill loyalty.

And giveaways and bonuses should not replace high quality. You want your customers to come back primarily because of your terrific products and service, not because they want to fly to Acapulco.

There are other ways to encourage customer loyalty that are more closely related to the best motivators: quality and innovation.

PRO FILE

Entrepreneurs: Jeannette Arsenault and Don Maxfield

Enterprise: Cavendish Figurines Ltd.

Jeannette Arsenault and Don Maxfield live in Prince Edward Island, Canada, where tourism is one of the primary industries. Many of the tourists who flock to the island every year come to visit the fictional home of Anne of Green Gables, made famous through the novels of Lucy Maud Montgomery. Loyal readers have purchased millions of these books, which still sell all around the world, even as far away as Japan. Jeannette, who had wanted to start her own business for some time, and Don, a draftsperson with some experience as a part-time entrepreneur, noticed that, although there's a wide variety of Anne memorabilia, there were no high-quality figurines of the characters from Montgomery's books.

Believing she had discovered a good opportunity, Jeannette quit her job as a government worker and she and Don started Cavendish Figurines. Neither partner knew anything about figurines, so they immediately enrolled in a 50-hour course on ceramic techniques and painting. Don, who had some artistic experience from his drafting business, quickly took to the art. Later, when they were ready to hire employees, they trained local people in the many steps of figurine production, including the detailed hand-painting that each item requires.

Today, Jeannette and Don employ six people full-time. This year's sales totalled 1,500 figurines (they sell for $190 to $270 each), which is double the volume of their first year. From the start, they planned for early and rapid expansion and they're ready to produce more than 3,000 pieces per year. At their current rate of growth, they'll soon be at capacity.

Cavendish Figurines Ltd. is rolling along very well, but it isn't by chance. Jeannette and Don have been very careful to build customer loyalty in their planning. "Instead of offering single pieces, we create collections," says Jeannette. "That way, a customer who buys one piece of a collection will be motivated to buy the remainder of the collection. And we do something most figurine companies don't do. When a customer buys the first piece of a numbered collection—for example, number 300—we guarantee that their subsequent pieces will also be numbered 300, so when their collection is complete, all the pieces in it will have the same number."

If the first piece of a new collection sells well, Jeannette and Don can more easily predict future sales of the remainder of that collection. That allows them the lead time to adjust production accordingly.

Entrepreneurs value and nurture customer loyalty

Jeannette Arsenault's and Don Maxfield's strategy for developing loyal customers doesn't involve unrelated bonuses or incentives. They simply provide a quality product in a field—Anne memorabilia—where customer interest is already high. And if the first piece of a new collection sells well, Jeannette and Don can easily predict future sales of the remainder of that collection, and adjust their production time accordingly.

 Entrepreneurs work smarter, not just harder

Strategic planning

By introducing numbered collections, Jeanette Arsenault uses using strategy. In her case, she asked the question, "Can I build customer loyalty selling numbered collections?"

Strategic planning is simply a matter of preparing your venture as well as you can for predictable future events. To do that you have to know how to predict those events, and you also have to know what you'd do if and when they happen. Most importantly, you have to know where you'd like your venture to go in the future, and why.

Remember your first car? Let's return to it one more time. You probably didn't know exactly how long that car would last. But you knew that the fan belt was worn and would last only a few more days; the tires looked like they'd last a month or so, and the engine was using a bit more oil every month. Finally, the mechanic advised you that the steering mechanism would likely become dangerous within six months at your current rate of driving. You had the facts. You wanted and needed a working car. All you had to do was plan accordingly.

Repair? Sell? Buy? Trade?

You were faced with a whole series of what-ifs. "What if I just keep driving the car and ignore all the facts?" Answer: First the fan belt will break and the car will be grounded. "What if the fan belt breaks? Do I fix it or sell the car?" Answer: It's pretty cheap to fix—better replace it now, before it breaks. What if I want to drive longer than a month? Answer: I'd better replace the tires.

As you worked your way through all the what-ifs, you were really forming a strategy to guide you in the decisions you had to make about your car. You've probably gone through exercises just like this one many times, if not with a car, then with some other major purchase or undertaking. When you ask, "What will I do if this or that happens? What do I want to happen and how can I try to make that happen?" you're engaging in strategic planning. Let's practice a bit of it right here and now.

EXERCISE 25

Task: To make a strategic decision
Objective: To practice strategic planning

This exercise assumes that you have not yet undertaken a venture; you're still exploring an option. For each option you're considering, list your relevant factors, priorities, and your most likely choice. The first example is a guide for the rest of the exercise. Try to list more options, priorities, and relevant factors than those given.

Imagine the company you work for is relocating to another country and you're invited to go with them for a higher salary and better position. Staying put means your job disappears.

You have the following options:

1. Go
2. Stay
3. Negotiate a separate deal
4. Go for a limited time

You need to consider the following factors:
- how much more money you will earn
- which country you're going to
- when you have to go
- health care
- other offers you may have here at home
- language requirements

_____

_____

_____

_____

_____

You may have these priorities:
- love traveling
- want continued high income
- want to broaden horizons
- want to maintain corporate loyalty
- want a safe neighborhood for family

_____

_____

_____

_____

Your best choice?

_____

Evaluation

You may have discovered that you already are a strategic planner. There's not much new here, except, perhaps, the way the format is organized. Strategy always involves options, factors, priorities, and decisions. So does your life. If you can see the point of this exercise, you can see how important strategy will be to your venture.

There's a Lot to Learn

In the last exercise you probably said to yourself, "But I don't have enough information to make these decisions!" Good for you! You recognize the importance of having enough good information. Too often entrepreneurs make decisions prematurely, based on too little information, often with catastrophic results. An important part of strategic planning is knowing how to get information and knowing where to get it from. If you need to know more about cars, you ask mechanics and salespeople; if you need to know more about real estate, you ask a realtor. If you need to know more about how to plan strategy for your venture, you ask someone like Larry Smith, who makes it his business to teach and advise entrepreneurs.

Good help is not hard to find

Larry Smith teaches entrepreneurship and economics at a major college. He also is president of his own consulting company, Essential Economics Corporation. He offers some advice about how to find good information:

"There are lots of people, called consultants, who will be happy to sell you their services for a good fee. I'm one of them. But if you're a new entrepreneur with a new venture, you probably don't have a lot of money to throw around. If you're in this league, you'll be happy to know that you can get some very good advice for free.

"In most areas, your regional or local government will employ someone, usually called an Economic Development Officer (EDO), whose job it is to help shape and guide economic development in your area. This person exists just to help and advise someone like you, and, unlike some expensive consultants, the EDO is used to walk-in traffic, just like you. You should be able to find your nearest EDO by calling your local chamber of commerce or checking with the your public library.

"In the past, EDOs were mainly charged with attracting industry to their community. But today, EDOs are much better trained to meet a broader range of business needs and often have to meet professional standards of certification.

"They can help you in a number of ways. They are excellent networkers—they can put you in touch with all kinds of people you'll need to know, from financial advisers to realtors to government officials. This type of networking grows, as each contact suggests more contacts and so on. Also, EDOs study trends, so they're aware of specific needs and challenges in your community or region and they'll make that information available to you, for free.

"There are other sources of information and help, such as your local college. To find out what they have to offer, you might go to their library. The librarian should be able to steer you to a specific department that might be able to provide you with studies, advice, or contacts—for a minimal fee, if there's any cost at all. You should ask if there are mentor programs available in your area. These programs can team you up with a seasoned entrepreneur who, over the course of the program, can provide you with a great deal of information and the benefit of years of experience.

"There may be a professional or industry association you could approach for advice and recommendations. For example, there are associations for restaurant owners, travel agents, manufacturers, and many other types of associations. These groups may well be able to recommend advisers with specific knowledge of your type of venture. You can check out directories of associations at your public library.

"Of course, you can get a lot of good help from your accountant or financial adviser, but you have to be careful how you choose such a person. Always check references to make sure you're getting high-quality and trustworthy service. Even if someone comes highly recommended, you still have to make sure that person knows and has experience with your type of business. Look for a kindred spirit and don't be shy; be assertive. When they offer specific advice, ask why. They should give clear answers. Beware experts who stand on their reputation and imply that you're ignorant.

"Remember, once you've found good outside sources of information and help, you can use them forever, not just for your immediate, specific needs. You can never have too much knowledge. The more you know, the more leverage you'll be able to bring to bear on your venture, and the better you'll be able to plan your strategy."

Don't be afraid to ask

As Larry Smith suggests, you shouldn't be afraid to ask questions of potential professional advisers. Here are some you could try:

1. How much do you charge for your services?

   You always have a right to know what you will be charged. If the price seems too high, you can leave without wasting more time. If you don't know whether it's high or not, ask how the price is calculated.

2. Are you familiar with my kind of venture?

You want someone who has experience with your type of venture. A financial adviser may have accumulated 20 years of professional experience without ever having set foot near the kind of venture you're proposing.

3. Can you provide references?

Most professional financial advisers are honest and reputable, but entrepreneurs do get ripped off from time to time. Get and check references. Rather than using the phone numbers provided for you, which can be a way of setting you up, find the phone numbers yourself, and make the calls.

4. How much help do you think I'll need, given what I've told you about my plans?

This answer isn't as important as asking "Why?" right afterward. Make sure an adviser can justify all his or her advice to your satisfaction.

These questions are just a start. The main thing to remember is that you're the customer, and you're paying the money, so you get to be picky.

KEY POINT Entrepreneurs always rely on high-quality advice and information

Good information provides you with options so that when you ask what-if questions, you'll be able to get some answers. The more what-ifs you plan to ask, the more information you'll need to answer them.

Of course, a big part of strategic planning is figuring out where you can and want to go, given what you've got to work with. Heading off trouble is another.

Planning strategy to head off trouble

What if your venture is going gangbusters? You'll be looking at a lot of what-ifs. For example, what if:

• you're hit with a major lawsuit?
• your suppliers dry up?
• your competition catches you by surprise with a lower price or better product?
• new technology renders your product or service obsolete?
• new import/export restrictions cut into your profits?
• a new labor code increases your costs?

Complex what-ifs require complex strategy. That's why entrepreneurs who are experiencing rapid growth take strategic planning so seriously. You probably aren't one of them yet, but you should have some idea how the pros plan strategy.

A strategy for success

Nowhere has growth been more dramatic in recent years than in the computer software industry. Effective growth management is neither a luxury nor an afterthought for companies competing in this market; it's a matter of corporate life and death. That's why Randall Howard and his partners at MKS spend so much time and effort on their strategic plans.

PRO FILE

Entrepreneur: Randall Howard

Enterprise: MKS (Mortice Kern Systems Inc.)

When Randall Howard graduated from his program of computer studies, the computer software industry was in its infancy, but he wasn't ready to start his own company just yet. For seven years he worked as an employee, honing his skills as a researcher and program designer, and paying close attention to how his employers ran their businesses. He found he enjoyed dealing with customers and helping them meet their specific needs. "That's probably when I learned about entrepreneurship," Randall reflects.

When he became intrigued by the idea of starting his own business, Randall and three partners came together to form MKS. "At first, we wanted to do what most other companies were trying to do—develop desktop publishing software," Randall says. "But we just didn't have the resources to pursue that kind of work—so, since we are all skilled programmers, we took contracts to do work for other companies and that's how we got off the ground." When MKS contracted about $2 million worth of work in its first 18 months, the partners began to see the considerable potential of their company.

"There was no great plan in place at that time," Randall explains. "We just plunged ahead and, as we worked for everyone else, we were learning what the needs of the industry were." As the partners worked on such projects as airline reservation systems and decision-support systems, they ran into a recurring problem. Software programmers didn't have enough good tools. Simply put, programmers use some software as tools to build other software.

Randall believed MKS had found its niche. While his partners continued to bring home the bacon through outside contracts, they supported Randall, who spent a year developing their first product. Less than three years after the company was born, the MKS Toolkit was launched with great success. MKS began to grow rapidly, and the need for serious planning soon became evident.

"I believe one of our greatest strengths has been our ability to anticipate problems before they became crises," Randall says. "The

▶ ▶ ▶ ▶▶▶▶

process of anticipation is really a large part of strategic planning. We tried a planning session on our own, and, although it was less structured than later sessions, we gained a great deal from just talking about potential problems." One of the problems they anticipated was their collective lack of business skills. They realized that they needed to augment their technical skills with business expertise, and so their first attempt at strategic planning addressed their need to focus on marketing.

To help them plan, they hired an outside facilitator. "Outside help can be really important in many ways," says Randall. "Facilitators can help you look at your business from a new perspective, and they bring objectivity to the process. They can help improve group dynamics, which is really important when partnerships are involved. Also, when you've hired someone to help you with strategic planning, that person tends to keep you on task. That person shores up your self-discipline, because it's really easy to let the day-to-day problems distract you from the planning process. But there are downsides, too," Randall cautions. "Consultants can help you make decisions but they can't make decisions for you—and they don't have as much at stake as you do. You have to trust your own instincts, too. That's really important."

Working with a strategic plan proved very useful and two years later MKS revisited the process, this time focusing on structure: the roles of management and shareholders. This time, they hired an industrial psychologist as a facilitator, and Randall feels the resulting plan was critical to their continued success.

"One of the most important outcomes was the decision to re-define the roles of shareholders," says Randall. "Because they have a stake in the company, shareholders sometimes feel as though they should be managers, even though they may lack managerial skills or any interest in management. As a result of that plan, shareholders felt better about doing what they were good at, rather than what they felt shareholders ought to do."

By now the planning process had become part of MKS's ongoing strategy for growth, and two years later the partners undertook their latest and most comprehensive strategic plan. Once again, they hired an outside facilitator, but they also took pains to change the process, as they had each time before. "It's really important to try new ways of planning and not to get stuck in a rut," Randall advises. This time they made the important decision to bring in board members from outside the company.

As a direct result of the latest plan, MKS's entire financial structure has been revamped, which, in turn, reflects a new organizational structure designed to accommodate further growth.

In spite of continued growth, MKS, which now has 85 employees, was able to create a leaner and more efficient operation as a direct result of its strategic plan, which allowed the company to eliminate some positions and give more control to teams. As with previous plans, the latest sets out ambitious goals for growth, but Randall is optimistic. "We have consistently exceeded our growth targets by 10 to 15%," he sums up, with obvious satisfaction.

What about me?

MKS is an extreme example of a rapidly growing company in a fast-growing field. You won't need such complex or thorough strategic planning just yet. But strategic planning can be reduced to a basic formula for your venture.

The whole exercise is really a matter of describing your venture in terms of its strengths, weaknesses, and goals. You could sum it up with a series of statements such as: "Given these problems, strengths, and circumstances and, given our goals, these courses of action must be taken." But the problems, strengths, and circumstances need to be known, before they can be used this way. Therefore, the process of strategic planning is really an exercise in learning. Here's a chance to learn more about this thing called strategic planning.

Strategic language

You may want to be familiar with the following terms, which tend to be found in strategic plans. For our purposes, each one is loosely defined by a series of questions:

Resource inventory and assessment

How much money do you have? How much credit can you get? How much do you owe? What are the terms of your loans? How many buildings and how much real estate do you own? How much equipment do you own? Is it good equipment? When will it need replacing? How many people with the right kinds of skills can you get? What are your greatest strengths and your greatest weaknesses?

Environmental assessment

What kind of world are you competing in? How is it changing? Who are your competitors now and who might they be in the future? What are the greatest threats to your venture? Are your raw materials going to get more expensive or cheaper? Is your market growing or shrinking? What is the political climate of the countries you deal with? How is new technology affecting your venture?

Learning strategy

How will you go about finding the information you'll need to answer all those questions above? What will you read? Whom will you talk to?

Venture strategy

What is the purpose of your venture? Where do you want it to go and why? What is your ultimate goal? What problems can you expect and how will you deal with them? How will you structure management? How large do you want to grow and how will you manage growth? Given where you want to go and given all the information above, what choices do you have?

Tasks

What do you have to do first? What do you do after that?

 Any planning is better than none

and

 Strategic planning lets you focus on the forest instead of the trees

What If There's a Recession?

Recessions aren't really a question of "what if?" They're more a question of "when?" If you're very young, you may never have witnessed, suffered from, or ridden through a recession. If you've once been bitten, you'll be twice shy. There isn't anything you can do to prevent a recession, but there are ways to avoid taking bigger losses.

Here are 10 recession survival tips:

1. Know that recessions will come. That can be difficult to believe if you've seen continuous growth and low interest rates for six or seven years straight, but believe it. If you know what to look for, you might see one coming and start adapting your production to the economic reality of the times. For example, during a recession, people tend to buy low-end items rather than upscale products. They go for the practical rather than the fashionable and they tend to hunker down at home, where they spend the least.

2. Listen to your customers. If they start to order less, defer payment longer and talk about growing inventory, look out! Consumers seem to know when recessions start and finish better than economists do. Pay attention to them. Listen to the talk on the streets.

3. Try to stay in the black. Pay as you go. Finance growth with profits. If a recession hits, you may have over-capacity, but at least you won't have a huge debt load. If you have to borrow, do it with the knowledge that low interest rates can rise and collateral can lose value. Beware lenders offering more money than you think you need. Lenders make money by loaning money. The less debt and the more collateral you have, the more attractive you'll be to lenders, so they'll come calling. However, be polite when you tell them "no thanks." You'll want to be on good terms with them when the tables turn.

4. Hang on to your customers by improving your service even more. Customers will tend to shop around more during a recession. Smother your clients with service: offer more, smile more, deliver to their door, and give them better terms.

5. Tighten your operation. Then, tighten it some more. Make sure you have the lowest possible costs and the lowest possible price and that you can compete. Take a hard look at everyone on your payroll. Anyone who isn't with the team will have to go.

6. Take more recession-proof contracts. No business is really recession-proof, but some clients are more protected than others. Governments, for example, are among the last to wake up to—or suffer from—the effects of a recession. Although government contracts can be difficult to nail down and even more difficult to manage, they can also be more secure in bad times. Try to get some business with local, regional, and national governments in the good times so they'll be there for you in the bad.

7. Take advantage of the low prices associated with recessions and stock up on new equipment, buy expansion property, or perhaps buy out a competitor.

8. These businesses traditionally suffer more during recessions: hotels and restaurants (especially expensive ones); lawn care and other convenience services; day-care services; real estate and everything associated with it; car and boat dealerships; fitness clubs; taverns and nightclubs; the airline industry; and the fine arts. These businesses tend to survive and sometimes even thrive in recessions: sales of used cars and trucks—in fact, used anything; repair services; auction sales; serve yourself, do-it-yourself, and U-fix-it services; educational- and training-related businesses; how-to books, magazines, and videos; counseling services; and low-end renovating services.

9. If you have to put the brakes on, put them on fast and firmly. Better to have a small piece of something solid than a large piece of instability. Take your sales staff off salary and put them on commission; renegotiate your lease. Don't wait until your line of credit is used up before taking action.

10. Try to have at least one or two people on staff, or in your network, who are old enough to have experienced a recession or two. If you're all in your twenties, you may be full of confidence and chutzpah, but you have a big hole in your collective experience. Times change, products and services change, and technology changes. But, as much as younger people often hate to admit it, some things stay very much the same. Nothing replaces experience, and a few sage heads can make the difference between growth and insolvency—if you listen to their advice.

◁ KEY POINT ▷ **Entrepreneurs plan for uncontrollable eventualities**

Am I an Entrepreneur or a Manager?

As your venture grows, you'll probably find that you're doing a lot more boring, everyday managing than you had hoped. It could be that the entrepreneur in you is getting restless. It's one thing to manage growth, and quite another to actually be a manager. By now, you'll realize that entrepreneurs are different from managers. True, one can be an entrepreneurial manager—that's the best kind of manager, in fact—but the skills required of a good manager often elude the entrepreneur.

EXERCISE 26

Task: To list the characteristics and skills of a good manager
Objective: To see if I am, or want to become, a good manager

In Part 1, list all the characteristics and skills you expect to find in a good manager. Describe the best managers you've ever known and picture them doing these things well. In Part 2, assess your interest and ability in each area. I've started off each part with a couple of examples:

Part 1

A good manager

   is patient and methodical _____

   is skilled at inventory control _____

   _____

   _____

   _____

   _____

   _____

   _____

   _____

   _____

   _____

   _____

   _____

Part 2

How I compare with a good manager

I am hurried and ad hoc _____

I loathe inventory control _____

_____

_____

_____

_____

_____

_____

_____

_____

_____

_____

Evaluation

Did you find that you fit the description of a good manager? Well, look no farther for your manager; it's you. Many entrepreneurs stay on as managers and are quite happy that way. But, if you found yourself wincing and moaning at each characteristic and skill, you should ponder your future as a manager. You may have to hire a good manager to take your place. Many entrepreneurs do just that. Some find they're happier doing research and development on new products; some like to hit the promotion circuit and drum up new business. Others discover that they only enjoy creating new ventures. This can be a sobering revelation.

Is that all there is?

As an entrepreneur, you may be on the go from morning to night, cajoling, entreating, promoting, and generally having a whale of a time proving that your own venture is viable. But, one day you may realize that, although your venture is doing very well, the thrill is gone. You may check in at the office only to be met with: a line-up of employees who want you to settle one problem after another; a salesperson trying to sell you a corporate credit card; the production boss, who wants a bigger lunchroom for her workers; and so on, until six o'clock. Although it's satisfying to work with a venture that you created, you may begin to ask yourself, "Is this all there is?"

The question to ask yourself is, "What more do I want?" Managers thrive on days such as the one you've just had. Their dream is to administer a business. They can be more or less creative, independent, and growth-oriented, but they are managers above all else. If you find yourself pining for the excitement of the days when you were first setting up your venture, you might do well to go out and find yourself a professional manager, so you can get back to entrepreneuring.

But you should know that if you hire a manager, you're going to have to let your manager manage. Stay out of the way unless you see the need to make a drastic change and replace your manager altogether. And be sure about this change, as it will have an effect on your employees. Entrepreneurship is about the long haul.

A lemon in three years, a plum in seven

It takes time to grow a successful venture—even with good advice and a lot of planning. There's a saying, "It takes three years to produce a lemon from a seed. It takes seven to produce a plum."

Most likely, it will take that long to get your venture really humming along and making good profits. It could take a bit less, but it could also take a lot longer. But, you'll barely notice the time flying by, because you'll be enjoying what you do.

In Chapter 7 you'll learn about some of the pitfalls of success and how to avoid them. But to conclude, here's a summary of the key points from Chapter 6.

 Summary

> **Entrepreneurs control the growth of their venture**
> **Entrepreneurs value and nurture customer loyalty**
> **Entrepreneurs work smarter, not just harder**
> **Entrepreneurs always rely on high-quality advice and information**
> **Any planning is better than none**
> **Strategic planning lets you focus on the forest instead of the trees**
> **Entrepreneurs plan for uncontrollable eventualities**

Surviving Your Venture

*Any landing you can
walk away from is
a good one*

à AVIATION SAYING

Entrepreneurs lead exciting and sometimes crazy, roller-coaster lives, but occasionally they wonder if they'll survive all the excitement. Your enterprise could have you so busy you may regret ever having started. Or you may have become addicted to work and discover that those around you are suffering as a result. Either way, you need a reality check and that means taking stock of your life. In this chapter, you'll:

- improve your decision-making skills
- learn how and why to delegate authority
- have the opportunity to take a fresh look at your personal values and see how they relate to your venture
- learn to recognize and avoid some common dangers, such as stress and substance abuse
- learn how to understand and survive failure
- discover that, without the proper preparation, your definition of success can be stood on its head.

But, first, let's look at making decisions.

Surviving Making Decisions

No matter what kind of venture you're running, you'll be making decisions every day, sometimes even before your first cup of coffee.

You'll have:

- **Scheduling decisions**

 Picture this: Your day is booked solid, with some meetings dangerously close to others, when you find out that the client you've been trying to reach for days is now available today. Do you take the meeting? Can you reschedule someone else?

- **Administrative decisions**

  Which telephone system should you install? How do you renegotiate a lease on your building? How should you organize staff vacations? Whom should you hire to replace your receptionist? When should you call the collection agency on some overdue accounts receivable? Should you pick up a cake for your accountant's birthday?

- **Marketing decisions**

  This letterhead or that? This advertising brochure or that marketing video? Go after this small but rich group of potential customers or that large but low-income bunch?

- **Personal decisions**

  Should you go to your daughter's birthday or have dinner with your lawyer? Should you pave the driveway or buy a better car?

When you're nose to nose with so many decisions, how can you know you're making the right choices? You could be tempted to defer decisions indefinitely, perhaps hoping they'll go away. One or two might dissolve into thin air, but you can't assume this will work for most. You might start an endless round of consultations, postponing the inevitable, but sooner or later, you have to make a decision.

One employee, clearly bored with being consulted one more time, once said to an entrepreneur, "Listen, it's not my job to make decisions. Don't worry about us so much, just decide." Another piped up, "Yeah. I mean, sometimes you're right and sometimes you're wrong, but you're always the boss."

Making decisions can be so difficult that some people make their way right to the top of corporations without ever making one. They manage to get everyone else to do their dirty work for them. You don't have to work that way.

As a decision maker, you're faced with one main question: How do I know I have enough information to make the right decision? Although your circumstances are unique, there is a generic approach to decision making that can help.

The following exercise is designed to help organize your decision making. Not all decisions are as easy as the example in the exercise, but many can be settled using this model.

EXERCISE 27

Task: To use a decision-making model to make a simple decision
Objective: To improve my decision-making skills

Part 1

Pretend you have to decide which photocopying machine to get for your business.

First, you list what you want your photocopier to do for you: these are your criteria for selecting a copier.

It must:
- be able to produce excellent copies
- be fast—one copy per second or faster
- be able to collate at least 20 copies
- be able to handle large sheets of paper
- be able to make transparencies
- be reliable, durable, and come with a full warranty
- be reasonably priced
- be compact in size
- be able to enlarge and reduce originals
- have a local, quick-response repair service
- have a lease-purchase option.

Now, list your options and criteria on the grid below. Note prices as well as other specifics about each machine on the grid, so you can make precise comparisons.

You're really just defining the good points of each option and then adding up the points to see which one wins.

PHOTOCOPIER OPTIONS						
CRITERIA	A	B	C	D	E	F
top-quality copies	✔	✔	✔	✔	✔	✔
speed	✔	✔		✔	✔	✔
collating	✔	✔			✔	✔
large sheets	✔	✔	✔	✔	✔	✔
transparencies	✔	✔	✔	✔	✔	✔
reliable, durable	✔	✔	✔	✔	✔	
full warranty	✔	✔	✔	✔	✔	
reasonable price		✔	✔	✔	✔	✔
compact size	✔	✔	✔	✔	✔	✔
enlarging/reducing	✔	✔		✔	✔	✔
service and repair	✔		✔	✔	✔	
lease-purchase option	✔	✔	✔	✔	✔	✔

Evaluation

In our example, only option E met all the criteria, so that seems to be the best choice.

Part 2

Try using this grid the next time you have to purchase a TV, VCR, or any other major home purchase. If it works for you, use it when you're deciding whom to hire.

What do you have to decide? Write it down:

_____

_____

_____

_____

List all the criteria your choice has to meet, along with your options, on the grid:

CRITERIA	A	B	C	D	E	F

Evaluation

Although you may not have been able to make your decision solely on the basis of this exercise, you should be clearer about which options are best and why.

Next best?

It's a good idea to have a plan B or second-best choice. That way, if your first choice turns out to have some unpleasant surprises, you can quickly choose the next-best option. The grid method can help you rank these choices.

You and your gut

Don't overlook your instinct. If you have two equal options, ask yourself which one you feel is better. Then go with it. Also, if you just don't feel you can live with the choice that wins according to the chart, pay attention. Don't ignore your gut feelings.

Is it time to decide yet?

The longer you put off making a decision, the more time you have to collect information and fine-tune your decision—up to a point. Don't make a decision until you have to. If you don't need to decide whom you'll hire as your financial officer for at least two weeks, why make the decision now? If you choose before you need to, you won't have the benefit of new information that you might have discovered in the meantime that would have affected your decision. Of course, you can always try to change your decision, but this can be costly in more ways than one.

If you're the sort of person who simply must take sides no matter what, stifle this impulse. Learn to keep your options open. It's not impossible. Just hold them simultaneously in your mind and add positive and negative attributes to each as you proceed toward the time of decision. Then, decide, for heaven's sake! And don't second-guess your decision. Get on with life.

 Entrepreneurs are skilled decision makers

Delegate or Pay the Price

One of the quickest ways to jeopardize your venture is to fail to delegate or to delegate improperly. Welcome to one of the toughest tasks you'll likely have as an entrepreneur.

Face it. You just can't do everything. You have to let others carry some of the load. In some cases, that will be easy. If you have people on your team who are already doing things you simply aren't capable of doing, you won't be too tempted to stick your nose into their areas of expertise. But, if you have to delegate to someone else what you like doing, such as writing or marketing, it's not going to be easy.

How to delegate

You've learned quite a bit about delegating already, in the sections on team building. Most of what applies to teams applies to individuals, but here's one more kick at that can. Pick the best people for the job, brief them thoroughly (we talked about communication in Chapters 2 and 5), and turn them loose.

DO: Let them do the job in their own way.

DON'T: Hover.

DO: Praise their efforts, even if it's not exactly what you would have done.

DON'T: Attempt to improve their work by criticizing: "You call this good work?"

DO: Give them the authority to do the job and stick to your decision.

DON'T: Secretly have someone else waiting in the wings, just in case.

DON'T: Undermine their authority by taking credit for their work.

DO: Encourage them to take risks and try new ways of doing things.

DON'T: Berate them if their risk fails.

DO: Say "Now we know how not to do something, and that's valuable."

To keep it, you have to give it away

One of the most difficult and intangible responsibilities you'll have as an employer is employee morale. It may seem that one day, your employees want to have you canonized, and the next, they want you drawn, quartered, and hung from the four corners of the lunchroom. There are a number of things you can do to keep up morale, such as profit-sharing programs, employee parties, and awards of merit. But the best approach, by far, is to empower your employees with authority. Give them a taste of what keeps you going.

By delegating authority and responsibility to your employees, you're giving them a reason to stick with you and your venture. The more they feel they're making a difference to the success of your venture, the more loyal they'll be. Be free with praise, especially in the company of outsiders. Remember, everyone knows this is your venture, so whatever makes the venture look good makes you look good. If you always hand the praise and glory to those who work for you, it will always make you look better than if you try to grab it for yourself.

Empowered employees provide you with more time to be a champion of the cause, to get out and hustle more business, and to raise your venture's profile. Empowered employees are going to be entrepreneurial employees. They'll take you and your venture to places even more exciting than you thought possible.

Entrepreneurs never do themselves what others can do for them

Becoming a better decision maker and learning how to delegate properly will go a long way in helping you survive from day to day. But, surviving won't necessarily head off disaster. You could be a great decision maker, with empowered, satisfied employees, and still be trying to climb the wrong mountain. What happens if it all starts crumbling around you? How can you survive failure?

How Do You Define Failure?

You might say that a failed venture is one that has gone bankrupt and ceased to exist. Hard to argue with that. Success, then, would be a venture that's making money. Sounds good. You might conclude that an entrepreneur always wants to avoid failure and achieve success. We could stop right here. However, let's draw some facts from a few profiles in this book.

Harold Warner considers himself a failure as a real estate developer, but says it was the best day of his life when he realized that fact because it forced him to get into ballooning. Peter Dalglish isn't a successful lawyer; it's a good thing because if he'd been a successful lawyer, the world wouldn't have Street Kids International. After making millions, Kaaydah Schatten lost it all; then she went ahead and made millions again. In fact, failure, like success, is a highly subjective term.

Banks and financial institutions know what they mean by failure and success, but how you define these terms is more important. Consider the following working definitions for now:

> *Success: achieving a goal*
> *Failure: falling short of a goal*

Remember the archer?

You'll recall the story of the archer in Chapter 2. Because he painted the target around the arrow, he had a bull's-eye every time. But was he successful? It all depends on what he was trying to accomplish. If his goal was to teach a lesson about goals, he succeeded. But if he intended to be a skillful archer, he only appeared to be successful.

You can't really know if you're a success or failure unless you know what you're aiming at.

Failure and setting goals

How you set your goals and objectives will determine how you evaluate your success. Consider the following example of two entrepreneurs who have set up identical ventures. The first one (let's call her Entrepreneur A) wants to get rich quick and the second (let's call her Entrepreneur B) aims for slow steady growth. Here are their first-year reports:

Entrepreneur A

Goal and Objective: To make a million dollars within one year
Startup: Completed within limits of capitalization
Accomplishments: team assembled; staff hired; production on line; distribution network established and operating; customers satisfied; growth steady at 20% per year
Gross sales: $500,000
Profit: 0
Loss: 0
Personal assessment: failure

Entrepreneur B

Goal: To service 10% of total market within 10 years
Objectives:
  First year:
  • to reach $500,000 in sales
  • to break even
  Second year:
  • to expand to 2% of market
  • to make a profit
  Subsequent years:
  • to grow at a rate of 20% per year
  • to increase market share by 2% each year
  • to increase profit margin to 10% or more
Startup: Completed within limits of capitalization
Accomplishments: team assembled; staff hired; production on line; distribution network established and operating; customers satisfied; growth steady at 20% per year
Gross sales: $500,000
Profit: 0
Loss: 0
Personal assessment: success

Who is more successful?

In every objective sense, A is just as successful as B. But because of the way A set her goals, failure was likely. She took little satisfaction in accomplishments along the way, because her ultimate goal was not being achieved. If her family and friends were expecting the big payoff, they, too, may feel that A failed. Her self-confidence and self-esteem will have suffered and she may go into the second year disillusioned and dispirited.

Entrepreneur B, on the other hand, had an ambitious but attainable goal, and a clear set of short-term objectives. She experienced success with each objective reached and, by the end of the year, could feel justifiably proud of the success of the first year of operation. Her financial backers will be happy and will likely be ready to jump in with more money should she need it. Her family and friends will be impressed at her ability to meet expectations and will likely be more supportive as she embarks on her second year of operation. Her self-confidence and self-esteem have likely grown with every objective she's met and she will likely go into the second year eager and energized.

 Failure and success are in the eye of the beholder

Creating the opportunities for success

So much depends on your ability to predict your performance and the performance of your enterprise that it's important to create opportunities for success in the way you set your goals and objectives. Allow yourself to succeed. To take satisfaction from small accomplishments, you have to predispose yourself to accept them as accomplishments and not merely requirements of the job.

Here's an exercise that can help you become more positive and success-oriented.

 EXERCISE 28

Task: To see how success-oriented I am
Objective: To become more success-oriented

Part 1

Look at the following list of everyday problems entrepreneurs might encounter to see how they can be viewed as opportunities for success or, on the contrary, reasons to get depressed. Check which view you're more likely to take: ▶ ▶ ▶ ▶▶▶▶

PROBLEM	OPPORTUNITY FOR SUCCESS	REASON TO GET DEPRESSED
Flat tire	___ let team work on own ___ nap while waiting for repair ___ learn to change tire ___ use cellular phone to return calls	___ late for work ___ more expense ___ get dirty ___ calls are backing up
Employees absent	___ give other employees a chance to try different tasks ___ tighten morale by pulling together in tough times ___ do their jobs yourself	___ twice as much work ___ extra work lowers morale
Lose contract bid to closest competitor	___ evaluate bidding process ___ evaluate competition ___ double effort on next bid	___ another lost contract ___ superiority of competition ___ start over
Client's check bounces	___ make new arrangement for payment ___ evaluate accounts receivable ___ tighten up selling practices	___ get nasty on phone ___ fire somebody
In summary	___ a day full of successes	___ a day to forget

Evaluation

How many responses did you check in the left column and how many in the right? If you checked more in the left column than the right, you're on the right track. You see problems as opportunities to succeed. If you checked more responses in the column on the right, you'd better give yourself a shake or your venture could be a short and painful experience.

Part 2

Settle down at the end of a typical day and make a list of the problems you encountered and how you dealt with them. Then evaluate your response in terms of success and failure.

PROBLEM	YOUR RESPONSE	SUCCESS OR FAILURE?
_____	_____	_____
_____	_____	_____
_____	_____	_____

PROBLEM	YOUR RESPONSE	SUCCESS OR FAILURE?
_____	_____	_____
_____	_____	_____
_____	_____	_____
_____	_____	_____
_____	_____	_____
_____	_____	_____

Evaluation

Did you have a day of successes or failures? If you thought of something as a failure at the time it was happening but now see it as a success, you're like many entrepreneurs. It's often difficult to view a problem in a positive way when you're in the middle of it. But if you can turn it around in your mind later, you're on the right track. Daily problems are a fact of life. Since they're inevitable, it makes much more sense to use them to your advantage—in terms of your enterprise and your sense of self-confidence.

 Entrepreneurs create success

To survive, change your perspective

Sometimes you need only to put your venture in perspective to move it from the failure column to the success column. Even if your venture leads to financial losses, you won't have wasted your time if you grew through the experience and learned how to do it better next time.

 Entrepreneur: Ross Colquhoun

Enterprise: Strata

Ross Colquhoun built his furniture manufacturing company, Strata, over a period of 10 years, during which his unique and critically acclaimed designs sold well. When Strata began to crumble under a recession, Ross was determined to survive the experience. He closed his retail storefront and began to concentrate on office and computer workstations for the commercial market. He downsized his factory payroll and took risks on long-shot contracts.

With each strategic turn, he moved from one building to another, renovating and remaking his surroundings as he went. Eventually, he moved his residence into his factory, which is where he was living when Strata was forced to close its doors. ► ► ► ►►►►

The recession that killed Strata also killed the market for medium-sized industrial space. After creating a living space for himself in a corner of the building, he began to use the materials left over from Strata to renovate the factory and turn it into unique apartments. "All I had was this classic old building and a pile of debt," Ross says. "So I thought, 'If I like to live in this kind of building, maybe others would too.'"

"Although I owned the building, I never thought of myself as a landlord until now," Ross remarks, as he hefts another piece of dry-wall into place. He had plenty of experience in renovations, having personally ripped up floors and walls, and installed plumbing and electrical fixtures in more than one old building. With these skills, and his well-developed artistic sense, Ross was the ideal person to create a whole new kind of living space. He found a financial partner who shared his own vision of factory living and together they plunged into the unknown.

It's been a white-knuckle adventure all the way. Building permits, planners, and tenants all had to be dealt with. But today his factory is five large apartments, complete with proud tenants, and the mortgage is covered "with a little bit left over." Being a landlord and interior designer wasn't part of Ross Colquhoun's game plan, but his eternal optimism and eye for innovation have made him a survivor, where many have fallen by the wayside.

 Entrepreneurs never give up

Surviving Success

You may not believe that success is something you have to survive. But consider the following scenarios:

Scenario 1

You've just completed another big deal and realized a healthy margin of profit. Things are looking good. You check your six-month sales projection and see that you are actually getting rich! It feels good. It makes you want to do more deals and start spending some of that money. Your bank balance says "Go for it!" So, you do. You decide to take the afternoon off and buy a car.

Later that day you roll up your driveway in your new convertible—just in time to see your spouse and children, suitcases in hand, getting into a cab. The last thing you hear your spouse say is, "My lawyer will be calling you."

Scenario 2

Imagine you've just received your share of your latest deal and you've never seen that much money before in your life. Why, you could pay off the house and car and still have enough left over to buy another house and car and still have some left over! You decide to stuff your pockets with an outrageous amount of cash and have some fun.

Later on, you're partying with high-flyers like you and someone offers you some cocaine. Your friend says, "It's expensive but it's not addictive. It's really no big thing." You find out your friend was right, it really does make you feel good—and powerful and in control. And it really is expensive, but, hey, you've got the money now and you know your limitations.

Twelve months later you're sitting on an apple box in the middle of your living room, watching the furniture company repossess your last possessions. You're broke, your partner has left you, and you've added alcohol to your cocaine addiction.

Scenario 3

You can't believe how much you love work. The more you work, the more you love it and the more money you make. You find out that you actually like working on Saturday and Sunday, too, and that the late nights seem to agree with your particular work habits. You haven't got time to exercise much—okay, at all—although you're sure it's a good thing to get started on someday. Food? Oh, you're eating all right—mostly restaurants and fast food, but you feel pretty good and you will definitely stop smoking next January. Okay, so you're a bit overweight. It's no big deal. Besides, you're you. You're not like everybody else and your bank account proves it. Whoa! Look at the time! You'd better run, or you'll be late!

"Who was he?" a doctor asks in the emergency room, as you and your gurney are wheeled down to the morgue. "I don't know," replies a nurse, "but he had a pile of money on him and you should have seen his watch! You know, he couldn't have been a day over 40!"

Take your pick

There are lots of ways to mess up your life. If you add financial success to any of them, you can speed up that process considerably. Which scenario above could be yours? Divorce? Drugs? Death? If any of them seem familiar, it's time for a wakeup call. You've learned how to become successful by learning from the mistakes of others. Don't stop now. Successful entrepreneurs fall into all three traps all the time. Learn from their mistakes.

You need to know what makes you happy. What are your priorities in life? Some people think they know, when they don't. For example, some poor souls work for years thinking that retirement is where it's at only to discover, once they do retire, that they really enjoyed their jobs. Others think work is what makes them happy when really, it's the time they spend with their families. Martha Sturdy knows what makes her happy.

PRO FILE

Entrepreneur: Martha Sturdy

Enterprise: Martha Sturdy (Fashion Accessories)

When Martha Sturdy was in high school, she was more interested in art than in business. "I just liked to make things. I sewed my own clothes, for instance," she says, "but it never went any farther than that." Ten years later, Martha found herself divorced with two children and working in a bank to make ends meet. She realized that if she was going to do something with her life she had better get started. So she began to design jewelry.

"It could have been shoes, for that matter," Martha reflects, "but I got started in jewelry. It wasn't so much about business as it was about art. I was more interested in the designing than the selling." But sell she did, and her unique designs became the talk of the fashion industry. She calls her work wearable art. "I have one piece—you may have seen it on the cover of Vogue—that weighs five pounds! Now, there's no way you can consider that a piece of jewelry. It's art!" says Martha of her remarkable fashion accessories.

Her business outgrew her house, so she moved into a new full-time location, where she could both manufacture and showcase her products for customers. Soon her sales were in the millions of dollars and she was famous. But fame is fleeting and you're only as good as your last show. "Now, it's 'What have you got for me this time?'" says Martha. "I have to keep coming up with new stuff all the time."

For some people, life in Martha's fast lane would be overwhelming and they would succumb to the stress. But Martha, who has since remarried, goes to great pains to keep an even keel. She doesn't fall for any of that fame stuff and she knows where her priorities lie. "If I didn't have my husband and my family as well as my work, it wouldn't be worth it. You've got to have it all to keep a balance. These people who work 18 hours a day are just hiding from life. Really."

EXERCISE 29

Task: To clarify my personal priorities in life
Objective: To be happy with success

Copy each of the following phrases onto individual cards and then arrange them in order of importance to you.

making money
my family's well-being
cutting deals
driving my car
spending time with my mate
spending time with my child(ren)
cooking dinner
eating dinner with my family
peace of mind
hanging out with friends
making love with my mate
great food
hiking (camping, fishing, touring) alone
hiking (camping, fishing, touring) with friends and family
financial freedom
going on dates
good health
sharing a good bottle of wine with my friends (or mate)
helping my child(ren) with their homework (project, bicycle, problems)
running a successful business
snuggling with someone I love
solving business problems
my hobby
looking attractive to others
playing sports
being respected by rich or influential people
being able to retire young
being able to look myself in the eye in the mirror
being able to fall asleep easily and sleeping well
holidays
having the respect of my family and friends
partying
drinking alcohol
my religion
travel
other

_____

_____

_____

Evaluation

It isn't easy figuring out our priorities. Worse yet, it's very hard to admit what our priorities should be, when we act quite differently. Now that you've arranged your priorities through this exercise, copy them out here in numbered order in your own words. Refer to them from time to time, just to remind yourself.

1. _____
2. _____
3. _____
4 _____
5. _____
6 _____
7. _____
8. _____
9. _____
10. _____
11. _____
12. _____
13. _____
14. _____
15. _____
16. _____
17. _____
18. _____
19. _____
20. _____

21. _____
22. _____
23. _____
24. _____
25. _____
26. _____
27. _____
28. _____
29. _____
30. _____
31. _____
32. _____
33. _____
34. _____
35. _____
36. _____
37. _____
38. _____
39. _____
40. _____

 Entrepreneurs keep their priorities straight

As far as can be known, no one's last words have ever been, "I wish I'd spent more time at work."

Remember what you really enjoy in life. As an entrepreneur, you're likely deriving most of your satisfaction in life from pursuing your venture. That's what you value. If you're already happy with your enterprise, house, neighborhood, and friends, why change them? You're already happy.

Money can be spent on a lot more than houses, cars, and boats. It can be spent on investments which you can then shepherd into capital gains as a different kind of entrepreneur. You can also finance other ventures and share in the excitement of others' successes. Not least of all, money can be spent on endowments to colleges, scholarships, and charities. It's not guaranteed, but you'll likely derive a good deal of satisfaction from spending your money this way.

Take time

As an entrepreneur you've already discovered the most valuable asset you have—time. Why not spend some of your money buying time—the time to do things, to spend with people you enjoy and respect. With time, you can travel, expand your horizons, continue your studies in any subject, and do the same for your family. But it's not easy to spend time. You'll find it very hard to avoid getting involved in other ventures. After a while, you may well find that you'd rather be entrepreneuring than doing anything else.

If you're just starting out, as you likely are, and you already have a well-balanced life—don't abandon it now. You can become an entrepreneur at the same time as you hang onto what you know is the source of your well-being. You can set your own rate of progress and you should never abandon your own good sense of what's right for you.

Our society doesn't need any more single-minded overachievers, all blindly plunging headlong toward success. We do need a society of balanced entrepreneurs—individuals who are happy being who they are, and who are making the world a better place by being happy in it. You'll be a welcome addition to that world.

Here's a summary of the key points in Chapter 7.

 Summary

    Entrepreneurs are skilled decision makers
    **Entrepreneurs never do themselves what others can do for
       them**
    Failure and success are in the eye of the beholder
    Entrepreneurs create success
    Entrepreneurs never give up
    Entrepreneurs keep their priorities straight

Toward an Entrepreneurial Society

"Some see things as they are and say, 'Why?' I dream things that never were and say, 'Why not?'"

& ROBERT F. KENNEDY

Now's the time to explore the new world you're just entering—a world of people who help solve their community problems and challenges by redesigning their own lives, and whose optimism and positive energy splash onto everyone they contact. In this chapter, you'll:

* learn how entrepreneurship is being taught
* learn that you're part of a phenomenon that is a growing trend
* meet a wide variety of unusual entrepreneurs.

In the previous seven chapters, you've met many people from whom you can learn a great deal about business ventures. You may find the people profiled in this chapter surprising in their diversity and their nontraditional enterprises. Among them, you'll meet a salaried entrepreneur, a part-time one and one whose physical challenges haven't dimmed his entrepreneurial zeal. Most importantly, you'll see how these people are changing their communities for the better, through their entrepreneurship. You'll also see how your initiative can benefit your own community, while at the same time supporting your own dreams.

You're Not Alone

You are part of a revolution in education. By taking up the challenges and rewards of running your venture, you're part of a new wave of change-makers. The flower children of the 1960s with their positive thinking and optimism were often accused of trying to change the world, while others affirmed the status quo and railed against what they saw as the arrogance and naiveté of that generation.

In the context of enterprise, those same dreams are now more acceptable. Through your entrepreneurship, you really will be helping to change the world, although you needn't concern yourself with such lofty motivation; just be yourself and forge ahead.

Entrepreneurship education: The cutting edge

There are many entrepreneurs, like Peter Dalglish or even Mother Teresa, for example, who measure their growth and success in terms of human and societal development. Some of them find innovative ways to sell entrepreneurship, itself.

PRO FILE

Entrepreneur: Gary Rabbior

Enterprise: The Canadian Foundation for Economic Education

If you met Gary Rabbior in a group of entrepreneurs, you'd notice how well he fits in and how naturally others relate to him. His enthusiasm and energy are contagious, and he's a masterful communicator. To him there are no problems without inherent opportunities and his only regret is that there isn't time to pursue them all. As he bounds off to his next appointment, you may be left wondering just what it is he's selling.

Like most entrepreneurs, Gary is selling an innovative new product. Like most, he didn't create it from scratch, but he has shaped it and put his own stamp on it. Most importantly, he found all kinds of new ways to package and sell it. His product, and the product of the nonprofit Canadian Foundation for Economic Education (CFEE), which is affiliated with its American counterpart, the National Council on Economic Education, is economic education.

Unlike most entrepreneurs, Gary, as executive director of CFEE, is a salaried employee. Unlike most salaried employees, however, Gary resists continual pressure to sell his entrepreneurial skills to the highest bidder. He isn't in it for the money. "I can't think of any other work that would offer me the kind of challenges on the cutting edge of something as new and important as those I'm pursuing right now," he says, as he races for a plane that will take him to any one of dozens of speaking engagements throughout North America. There, he will captivate audiences with his vision of a more entrepreneurial world, made possible through education.

Under Gary's direction, CFEE played a key role in developing a curriculum in entrepreneurship education that is the envy of the world. Working with governments and business, he has created innovative print and video resources that are used by thousands of

▶ ▶ ▶▶▶▶▶

educators throughout North America and around the world.

A few years ago, there were no credit courses in entrepreneurship education at the high school level. Today, largely due to Gary Rabbior's efforts, thousands of high school students have already benefited from innovative credit courses in entrepreneurship and the number is growing by thousands each year. "I can honestly say this is the best course I have ever taken," reports one student. Another says, "This course has changed my life."

"This is powerful stuff," says Gary. "Entrepreneurship education has the potential to revolutionize education over the next 10 years. It is as liberating for teachers to teach entrepreneurship as it is exciting for students to rediscover and nurture their own spirit of adventure."

Entrepreneurial teachers

Who's the best person to teach entrepreneurship? You might think an entrepreneur would qualify. Some might, but most lack the skills required. You recall the importance of team building and how it's critical to find the right people for the right job. If you need something sold, you hire a skilled salesperson; if you need a company logo, you hire a graphic artist; if you need something taught, it makes sense to get a skilled teacher. If you don't believe this, try teaching a class of 30 young people for a day or even for 30 minutes, and you'll have more appreciation of the skills required.

Every day good teachers use creativity and innovation to sell knowledge to their students. They try new lesson plans and new ways of designing tests and exercises. They are persistent and never give up on someone's ability to learn. Their product is a pupil who likes to learn. Teachers of entrepreneurship report that it is the most enjoyable course they've ever taught, in part, because it encourages them be the kind of teacher they've always wanted to be—a creative, innovative facilitator of learning.

Group enterprise: Cooperative entrepreneurship

As they try new ways of achieving their goals, entrepreneurs are continuing to expand the boundaries and applications of entrepreneurship. Some people, such as Carol Livingstone, prefer to work in groups.

PRO FILE

Entrepreneur: Carol Livingstone

Enterprise: The West Point Lighthouse

She can see the lighthouse from her kitchen, and every time she glances out the window at it, Carol Livingstone is reminded of how the venture all started.

Carol and her neighbors, who make up the tiny population of West Point, live on the shore of an East Coast island. Carol is a former teacher, but her community has seen few economic opportunities beyond the traditional and precarious fishery. For many decades, however, the most prestigious and secure job in the community was that of the lighthouse keeper. That job fell victim to advancing technology when an automatic light was installed 30 years ago.

The light continued to serve passing sailors, but without a keeper, the lighthouse slowly began to deteriorate. The paint peeled, the vegetation grew wild and the buildings became the favorite haunts of young people, whose graffiti and trash bore mute evidence of their visits.

"It broke my heart to look out the window and see that lighthouse, which had been such a proud symbol of our community for so many years, fall into disrepair," says Carol. "I thought, 'There's nothing for anybody to do around here—so maybe we could make ourselves busy trying to restore the old lighthouse.'"

Carol found that she wasn't alone in her concerns, so she assembled a group of likeminded friends. Together they created a nonprofit development group dedicated to restoring the lighthouse.

They had a lot to learn about organization and bureaucracy. But through four to five months of tireless, unpaid work, they managed to get $54,000 of initial funding through the government. The volunteers then proceeded to oversee the restoration of the old lighthouse to its original splendor. And tourists began to arrive, drawn by the unique building.

"One of our members said, 'Well, if we're going to get tourists, we might as well sell them something. How about opening a chowder kitchen?'" Carol recalls. "Another said, 'Why not restore the old keeper's cottage and rent rooms?' That's how it all started to come together, with everybody making suggestions.

"Today, in a community of only 140, as many as 25 people a year find employment at the West Point lighthouse. Some work in the restaurant, where customers can enjoy a full menu, including chowder. Others work as tour guides, sell crafts, or operate overnight accommodations. Some years, the lighthouse features dinner theater, with local performers who entertain diners with tales and songs from West Point's maritime history.

"I'm a bit of a history buff," Carol confesses, "and it really makes me proud to see our history come alive in that old lighthouse. That something from our past should become such a large part of our economic future is very exciting for me."

Is there a "deteriorating lighthouse" in your community?

What about your community? Has technology left its mark in abandoned buildings, steam engines, or rail lines? Maybe you could spearhead a citizens' group that might restore something from your past and put it to some new and worthwhile use.

For example, in many parts of the world, railroads are being abandoned, leaving thousands of miles of old railroad lines to rust, unused. Some communities are beginning to recognize what a tremendous resource these railroads can be—as hiking and bicycling trails! The steel rails and ties can be recycled, leaving perfectly engineered roadways, bridges, and tunnels through countryside that is hidden from highway travelers. Where steam-driven locomotives once shrieked, now bicyclists pedal quietly along smooth, straight paths, far from the noise and danger of cars and trucks.

But converting old railroad lines to new uses doesn't happen by chance. It takes the efforts of interested citizens to champion the cause and see it through to completion.

In North America, railroads have become the stuff of nostalgia, but to the aboriginal people of North America, railroads mark a point in history when their culture and traditions were threatened with extinction. Meet a group of young entrepreneurs whose enterprise is focused on restoring their cultural identity.

Entrepreneurs: Mark Maltais, Donna Testawich, Dean Gladue et al.

Enterprise: The Northern Shadow Dancers

Mark Maltais had been in and out of school more than once before he was invited to take up studies at the local enterprise center. The same was true of most of his friends, who, as aboriginal Crees, also bore the psychological scars that, in part, result from the uneasy coexistence of native and non-native cultures in their part of the world.

They began under the mentorship of Garry Oker, their teacher at the center. An accomplished clothing designer, Garry had returned to his roots from the big cities of the east. He wanted to help his people revive, come to terms with their traditions, and take their places as modern economic warriors. Garry worked patiently with his young students, teaching them about their own culture as well as the world of business. Through him, the students began to learn traditional songs and dances.

Three years later, a group of his students, headed by Mark, Donna Testawich, and Dean Gladue, said, "Thank you very much. We can take it from here. We'll let you know if we need any help." Forming a dance troupe of young people, they called themselves The Northern Shadow Dancers.

The Northern Shadow Dancers are all students between the ages of 11 and 22, who operate a cooperative enterprise that is more than a means to make money. "We are the northern people, who are dancing in the shadows of our ancestors," explains Mark, president of the enterprise.

"We learn our songs and dances from the elders," says Dean, who's the vice-president, "and we learn how to perform them with respect, in the traditional way."

"And we make our own costumes," adds Donna, who's in charge of marketing. The Northern Shadow Dancers perform for schools, service groups, fairs, and exhibitions—and they're in demand. "We've just finalized arrangements for a European tour and for 10 days of performances at a major West Coast exhibition," Donna says.

Their venture is both innovative and profitable, and its owners are entrepreneurs in every sense of the word. But their management is more consultative, with everyone having an equal say in the decision-making process. "We make all our decisions as a group," says Mark. "The majority rules."

Last year the Northern Shadow Dancers, who are all still in school, earned $17,000—and this year that figure could easily double. Most of the money is pumped back into the venture, where it's spent on sound and lighting equipment, touring costs, and other expenses. The rest of the money is used to explore other business opportunities.

In their shows, the Northern Shadow Dancers perform and explain ancient dances and songs that help non-native audiences understand aboriginal traditions. Each performance includes a session in which members of the troupe, in full costume, answer questions from the audience about their dances, songs, and native traditions. "Our purpose isn't just dancing," explains Mark. "It's to spread the word about native people; to educate native and non-native people; to eliminate stereotypes and show that native people are really strong and proud."

As the Northern Shadow Dancers sign their latest touring contract, there's little doubt that they've used their knowledge of entrepreneurship to create a business. But it's clear that the same process also helped generate a much more profound outcome. They are using entrepreneurship to understand, preserve, and promote their own culture. In the process, they continue to grow in confidence, self-esteem, and in the knowledge of their own history and spirituality.

Entrepreneurs Teaching Other Entrepreneurs

Citizens of multiracial and multicultural societies are well aware of the problems of racial discrimination. For many entrepreneurs, race is a non-issue, but Ron Thomas uses entrepreneurship as a powerful tool to overcome prejudice in his own community. Ron isn't the head of a church, but he is something of a preacher on the subject of entrepreneurship.

PRO FILE

Entrepreneurs: Ronald and Marie Thomas

Enterprise: Thomas Discount Stores Ltd.

Ron Thomas had many years of experience as an employee in the clothing industry in a large city before he and his wife, Marie, started their own retail operation in a small remote East Coast community. As a black person, Ron found that "Racism and discrimination are like fly droppings. You can find them everywhere. However, one step up the ladder and all that is below you."

They had a tough time getting started, but, after five years of hard work, Ron and Marie had established the first black-owned discount clothing store in the history of that region. Ron began spending a good deal of his time helping other black people overcome the same obstacles he and his wife had encountered. "We used obstacles as stepping stones and forged ahead," says Ron. He showed other black businesspeople how to use existing agencies to get started in business, and how to open doors often closed to blacks. Ron likes to quote musician James Brown, "I do not want nobody to give me anything. Just open the door and I'll get it for myself."

Ron and Marie are retired now, but that doesn't mean they've stopped working. Ron continues to counsel anyone in his black community who needs help getting started in business, and he recently ran for district council, losing by only a few votes. But he isn't discouraged. "I believe it's important for the black community to pull together if we are to overcome the challenges that minorities face everywhere."

Society is home to all kinds of people, some more challenged than others. As you become more entrepreneurial, you'll find there isn't much that will stop you, once you've set your mind to a venture.

PRO FILE

Entrepreneurs: Thomas Reeves and Debbie Oickle

Enterprise: T&D Nurseries

Thomas Reeves and Debbie Oickle live in the Christmas tree capital of the world. Thomas had training in forestry and had worked in forest operations most of his life, and Debbie had bookkeeping skills, so it's not surprising that a nursery-growing operation was a passing notion for them.

But before they could turn their idea into a venture, Thomas was involved in an accident in 1983 that left him quadriplegic. At first, it looked like all their dreams were shattered. But, to Thomas and Debbie, no obstacle was too big to overcome.

In the occupational therapy department of the rehabilitation centre, Thomas was introduced to the mouthstick, a tool he can use to operate a computer. Although he wasn't trained on computers, he was motivated to teach himself, by trial and error. Debbie helped him with the basics of bookkeeping, and when he returned home, they decided to set up a greenhouse nursery, growing tree seedlings and bedding plants.

Debbie had a lot to learn by trial and error as well. Before the accident, Thomas had expected to do most of the physical work in the venture, but since that was no longer possible, Debbie had to learn how to drive tractors and do all the physical tasks.

Thomas keeps the records, does part of the bookkeeping, and sets up crop schedules. Debbie looks after the crops, oversees the employees, puts finishing touches on the bookkeeping, and does most of the maintenance. When purchasing equipment, they look for gear that's easy for Debbie and the employees to operate and repair. For example, their tractor is hydrostatic, which means there's one pedal for forward and another for reverse, with no shifting or clutching required.

Their perseverance has paid off. Several years after its startup, T&D nurseries is alive and thriving. During a recent economic downturn, their reforestation contracts all but dried up, but thanks to their hard work and quality products, the demand for their Christmas tree seedlings has remained strong and healthy—just like their venture.

If you're looking for an excuse to give up or not to try in the first place, you won't find any among practicing entrepreneurs. There are no limits to creativity or the human spirit.

The Entrepreneurial Society

Imagine a society in which everyone is an entrepreneur. What would such a place be like?

Among the most noticeable difference would be the positive atmosphere. Instead of dreading and bemoaning problems and the lack of opportunities, people would turn problems into opportunities. Instead of marching in the streets, demanding that someone else give them a job, people would create their own jobs and hire others—who aren't quite ready for their own ventures—to help them. Instead of making excuses for poor-quality products and lackluster service, people would take responsibility for their roles in ventures from coffee shops to industrial assembly lines. Instead of despairing about their futures in dead-end jobs, people would join forces with their employers to recreate their jobs and help their employers become more competitive.

In a society where everyone feels in control of their own lives, there would be much less litigation, as people would take more responsibility for their own risks and the outcomes of those risks. People would recognize how their decisions affect their individual futures—that they play the largest part in creating those futures. As a result, few people would see themselves as victims. Rather, they would see themselves as needing to develop more control over their lives.

You might ask, "With all these entrepreneurs around, who's going to do all the other jobs? For example, who's going to fix my teeth?" If you lived near Dr. Hilary Rodrigues, your dentist might be this entrepreneur.

PRO FILE

Entrepreneur: Dr. Hilary Rodrigues

Enterprises: His local community

When Hilary Rodrigues set up his dental practice in a remote northern community, the local citizens got more than they had bargained for. They got an entrepreneur with an eye for opportunity.

"When you see an opportunity, you really must take advantage of it," says Hilary, who has had quite an effect on his community, as he pursues one opportunity after another.

Jobs are scarce in remote communities, but when Hilary built a pharmacy next to his dental office, eight local people suddenly had full-time employment. Eight more people will work at a blueberry winery that he's currently completing. "Blueberries are a main export from the area," says Hilary. "I did some research and found out that our blueberries end up in another country where they are made into wine. It seemed to make more sense to keep the blueberries and export the wine," he says. Ever the innovator, Hilary has a number of spin-off ventures already in the piloting stage, including iceberg water and blueberry jams and jellies. Five more people will work at the restaurant that will be built beside the winery, and a tourist lodge will employ yet more local citizens.

Several years ago, he was elected mayor, and soon had plans underway to completely renovate the town's sewer and water services. He has since served on boards of programs designed to foster entrepreneurship among younger people, as well as helping established businesses develop new ventures.

Meanwhile, Dr. Hilary Rodrigues continues to practice his first profession, dentistry, while his community benefits from his part-time ventures. "I seem to be able to see opportunities where others don't," he says. "I just like to get projects started and then let someone else run them."

It's your turn

You know what it takes to be an entrepreneur, and you know how entrepreneurs approach life and its problems. Try one last exercise to see if you can picture what an entrepreneurial society would be like. To refresh your memory, here's a list of characteristics and skills that entrepreneurs bring to their ventures.

Entrepreneurs tend to be:

• self-confident

• self-starters who take the initiative

• optimistic and positive thinkers

• sensitive to opportunities

• creative thinkers and creative problem solvers

• good team builders and players

• motivated by the desire to accomplish things

• willing to take calculated risks

• community-minded

• involved in ventures centered on their interests and expertise.

EXERCISE 30

Task: To describe each character below in entrepreneurial terms
Objective: To imagine an entrepreneurial society

Imagine that you're having an ordinary day, going about your business in your city or town and you meet each of the following people. Imagine that they have shared your experiences in working through this book. How would each one be different as a result? The first two are done for you.

People in your community	As entrepreneurs, they
The grocery clerk	• love working with groceries
	• like dealing with people
	• are interested in learning every aspect of the grocery business
	• are as happy at work as they are at home.
The banker	• chose banking because they like working with people and finances
	• are always trying new financial services
	• have their own part-time venture— perhaps financial counseling
	• enjoy practicing better customer service
The plumber	
The day-care worker	
The high school teacher	

The politician

_____

_____

_____

_____

The restaurant waiter

_____

_____

_____

_____

The auto mechanic

_____

_____

_____

_____

The lawyer

_____

_____

_____

_____

The doctor

_____

_____

_____

_____

The shopkeeper

_____

_____

_____

_____

The government employee

_____

_____

_____

▶ ▶ ▶ ▶▶▶▶▶

Evaluation

In each case, you probably noted that the people in that role chose it because of their skills and interests. That's a big difference from the way things are now. Most people feel that either they have no real choice in what they do or they choose a career based on money and prestige. If they see each job as an opportunity for self-fulfillment, innovation, and creative problem solving, they'll be full participants in an entrepreneurial society.

Among aviators, it's an odd but well-known fact that pilots, when in control of their aircraft, rarely get airsick. As soon as pilots give up control to become passengers, they become as vulnerable to motion sickness as anyone else. The message is simple: If you have little or no control over your future, you may feel like a helpless victim, bounced around by the outside forces of day-to-day living. Life can be a frightening—and sometimes sickening—experience. But, as long as you're in control, the ups and downs of life become part of an exhilarating ride.

When you become an entrepreneur and take control of your life, you are creating an environment in which you're in charge of the trip and you pick your destination. As an entrepreneur, you can give your initiative full rein, riding it as far as your imagination leads you. From today on, you will create your own future. You won't rely on luck or on getting the right breaks.

If you believe that, through your efforts and initiative, you make your own breaks in life, this book has been worthwhile. The more you examine it, the more you will discover that your environment is largely a product of your own choices and decisions in life. Armed with self-knowledge and this book as a road map, you can set out to create your own future. Bon voyage!

Appendices

Ask an Entrepreneur: An Interview Guide

Feel free to copy the following two pages to fill in each time you interview an entrepreneur.

Name of entrepreneur: _____

Name of enterprise: _____

Date of interview: _____

Questions to ask:

1. Are you the sole owner or a partner in this venture? _____

_____

2. What product or service do you sell? _____

_____

3. Why did you start this venture? _____

_____

4. Why did you think there would be an opportunity for this kind of venture? _____

5. Would you call yourself an entrepreneur? Why? Why not? _____

_____

6. Using this simple method of scoring (1 = very important; 2 = important; 3 = not very important), mark how important you think it is for an entrepreneur to:

___ have self-knowledge: likes, abilities, strengths, and weaknesses

___ have the ability to learn from mistakes and use experience
___ be self-confident and have self-esteem
___ be able to set clear, high goals
___ need to achieve
___ want to be rich
___ be persistent
___ be a risk taker
___ be a manager of risk
___ be a gambler
___ be a team builder
___ be a loner
___ be honest
___ work hard and be a self-starter
___ think positively and view failure as a learning experience
___ be a dreamer and a visionary
___ be an innovator
___ be an inventor
___ love life

7. What's the best thing about being an entrepreneur? _____

_____

_____

8. What's the worst thing about being an entrepreneur? _____

_____

_____

9. What kind of skills do you use most in your business? _____

_____

10. Which of these skills did you have to learn since starting your venture?

_____

_____

_____

Business Lingo

Accounts receivable: Money that is owed to you. Accounts receivable are included on a balance sheet under current assets. Even so, money that is owed can't be spent until it is received. Some entrepreneurs get into a cash-flow problem when they pay cash out faster than they receive it. One view of accounts receivable is reflected in this adage: "A sale is a gift until it's paid for."

Assets: Anything you own that either is money or can be turned into money. Assets include land, buildings, machinery, stocks, bonds, inventory, cash, patents, investments in other companies, and accounts receivable.

Bottom line: The figures at the bottom of the page that indicate either profit or loss. Also used, colloquially, to mean a concise summary of facts.

Business plan: A detailed plan for starting and operating a business. See also Strategic plan and Venture plan.

Calculated risk: A risk taken after careful planning.

Capital: Money or anything that can be turned into money.

Cash flow: Money flowing into and out of a venture.

Collateral: Assets that are used to guarantee the repayment of a loan or security.

Depreciation: The reduction in value, over time, of a fixed asset, such as a truck. At the time of purchase, a truck might be worth $25,000, but, due to wear and obsolescence, it might depreciate to half that value after two years. Depreciation also refers to the amount of value of a fixed asset that a business can deduct as an expense for tax purposes over a specified period of time.

Economic climate: The economic conditions under which a business operates: These include rates of taxation, economic growth, unemployment, and interest rates.

Equity: The portion of a business or asset that is owned. To have equity in a house is to have a claim on part or all of its value.

Gross income: Total revenue (income) before subtracting costs or deductions.

Interest rates: The rate at which interest is charged, expressed in a percentage. Prime rates are those charged to preferred customers.

Inventory: Unsold stock.

Liabilities: Debts.

Line of credit: A pre-approved loan, like an overdraft, often used to ease cash flow problems.

Market analysis: A description of a company's potential customers, their numbers, age ranges, buying preferences, and so on.

Mission statement: A concise, sometimes lofty, vision of a venture's goal.

Net income: Also called profit. It's the money left over when you deduct your business expenses and taxes from your total income.

Proprietor: Owner.

Revenue: Income.

Sole proprietorship: A business with one owner.

Strategic plan: A business plan that involves planning for growth and potential problems.

Venture capital: Money that is used to invest in new ventures.

Venture plan: A business plan that involves innovation and risk.

Wholesale price: The price a retailer pays for a product.

Sample Venture Plan

The profile of the Lang & Ackroyd Band, on page 121, includes a description of a venture called Little Johnny Records. In thinking back over that venture, my partner, Mary Ackroyd, and I began to explore the possibility of a new venture, based on opportunities that have arisen since the demise of vinyl albums and the growth of the audiocassette and compact disc (CD) market.

This new venture, a side venture of our current company, Lang & Ackroyd Productions, is one where we can learn from our past mistakes, retain the musical quality of our earlier venture, and put our extensive recent experience in TV and video production to good use.

Although venture plans don't have a standard length, most have a similar sequence and structure. We have attempted to present our plan in the simplest and shortest format. Obviously, all plans are unique. In using the following one as an example, be aware that many plans are much longer and more complex.

Our submission to the Bank of New Venture Capital would also include financial statements of the parent firm, Lang & Ackroyd Productions, as well as any details related to collateral and personal financial statements.

Lang & Ackroyd Productions

proposes a new venture:

LJ Music
A re-recording and re-issue of

"Lang & Ackroyd: Fiddle & Guitar"
18 all-time favorite fiddle and guitar tunes!

For distribution through direct-response television sales

Presented to

The Bank of New Venture Capital

by

Jim Lang and Mary Ackroyd
Owners and operators of
Lang & Ackroyd Productions

LJ Music Venture Plan

Table of Contents

Page

Executive Summary

We propose to market an instrumental musical recording called "Lang & Ackroyd: Fiddle and Guitar" through direct-response television marketing. The music will be 18 all-time favorite fiddle and guitar tunes.

This recording, on our new LJ Music label, formerly LJ Records, will be the re-mixed tracks from a previous recording that we sold through direct-response TV marketing. This time, it will be reproduced in audio-cassette and compact disc (CD) formats. It will be designed specifically for direct-sales distribution via a television commercial to be aired by selected broadcasters, who will participate according to standard per-item sales agreements.

Our competitive edge
- We have a proven product in hand.
- We have the benefit of experience in marketing this product, in this way (see below.)
- Through Lang & Ackroyd Productions, we are able to produce the required commercial at minimal cost.
- New direct-response marketing techniques allow us to set up LJ Music as a self-sustaining venture. Once it has been launched, virtually every aspect of its operation will be subcontracted, leaving the partners to their full-time pursuits with Lang & Ackroyd Productions.

Learning from mistakes
From our first attempt at direct-response marketing, we've learned:
- to choose only television stations with predominantly rural audiences
- to subcontract the filling of orders
- to avoid advance payments or deposits to television stations
- to schedule the promotion to match peak sales months
- to provide a longer how-to-order segment in the commercial
- to avoid CODs.

Financing
LJ Music will be a self-sustaining, wholly-owned subsidiary of our parent company, Lang & Ackroyd Productions, and will be operated by the same partners. We have calculated fixed and startup costs of LJ Music at $11,055. These costs include remixing and duplicating the first 3,000 units of the product, producing a television commercial to market the product, and establishing a direct-response network. Lang & Ackroyd

LJ MUSIC / page 1

Productions will underwrite approximately 50% of these costs. This submission is a request for financing the remaining 50%. Our cash-flow projections indicate that LJ Music would become self-sustaining and turn a profit in the second year of operation.

Market potential
LJ Music will be a modest undertaking. Our product is designed for a narrow market in select regions only. We are targeting a niche market buyer, identified as an aficionado of traditional fiddle and guitar instrumental music, in particular, and country music, in general. The customer is middle-aged or older, and lives predominantly in western rural North America.

Our customers will learn of the product through television commercials that will be aired by six stations serving predominantly rural markets. We will concentrate our promotion on the three peak sales months of January, February, and March. There will be repeat promotions during April, May, and June, for a total promotion period of six months per year, for three years. After the first year, we will consider expanding the operation to include six more stations.

Sales projections
Cassettes will sell for $12.99 and CDs for $16.99, plus $3 shipping and handling. January through March are peak sales periods, while April sales are likely to be half those of March. Sales in May and June, as the promotion period tapers off, will likely combine to equal sales in April. We expect sales of 80 cassettes and 40 CDs per station per month, in the peak months.

Sales projections: Year One

	JANUARY	FEBRUARY	MARCH	APRIL	MAY	JUNE	YEARLY
Cassettes	480	480	480	240	120	120	1,920
CDs	240	240	240	120	60	60	960
Total units/mo.	720	720	720	360	180	180	2,880

Based on our previous experience in direct sales, and on current market conditions, we anticipate sales of approximately 2,000 audiocassettes and 1,000 CDs in the first year. This would return gross revenues of approximately $50,000 per year, with a profit of approximately $5,000 after one year, and $15,000 after two years.

Costs

We anticipate costs of approximately $45,000 in our first year. Second-year costs would shrink to $35,000 and sales would remain constant.

The competition

A survey of direct-response marketing firms and television stations indicates that no similar current or planned product will be competing directly with ours, in our sales territories, during the planned promotional periods. The large national and international direct-response companies indicate no interest in niche market products, and offer no direct competition. Furthermore, we have the advantage of working through small regional television outlets, which are more receptive to our kind of product. With generally lower operating costs and a mandate to serve a local rural market, these stations will be more favorably disposed than their large urban counterparts to extend the promotion period, in spite of the relatively low volume of sales our product will generate.

The team: Lang & Ackroyd Productions

Lang & Ackroyd Productions is a consulting and communications company owned by Jim Lang and Mary Ackroyd. Our primary products are educational television programs and print and video resources for teachers. We also offer consulting services, including seminars and workshops related to entrepreneurship and business education, to educators, foundations, government agencies, and business associations. The financial summary of our last three fiscal years demonstrates that we are a viable company, with sufficient cash flow to meet our commitments as stated in this plan.

We bring 10 years of experience in the music business to the LJ Music venture. We have produced and sold four recordings, including one designed for direct sales. We broke even on sales of 1,800 units of the latter through a sales scheme very similar to the one detailed in this plan. Our experience in that venture allows us to plan for profit in this one.

Goal

Our goal is to sell a minimum of 3,000 units per year, over three years, for a gross profit of approximately $5,000 after our first year and $15,000 per year after that. After the first year, we will evaluate our sales to determine plans to expand to include additional television stations and their markets.

Market Analysis

Informal research

We have identified our market through direct feedback from our audiences during our years as a touring and performing group. Our customers are:

- male and female
- over the age of 40
- rural
- low to middle income
- previous purchasers of acoustic fiddle and/or guitar recordings
- previous customers of direct-response marketing promotions.

Formal research

To bring our research up to date, we contacted television stations WKSJ and CMYB, as well as Apex Distributing, which specializes in direct-response marketing. These organizations provided information that confirmed our own previous research. Since they're interested in pursuing business with us, they were happy to provide the information free of charge. They indicate that our projected sales to customers are likely on target. However, they caution that, although our market has remained stable, it is relatively small.

Resource Analysis

Cassette/CD production

We have selected Fastrax Studio for remixing and remastering the recording. Fastrax will provide good value, while employing the latest technology. The original tracks will be remixed and transferred to digital audio tape (DAT), for transfer to the cassette and CD formats. Fastrax will provide an in-house producer, Carol Cisco, who has worked with us before and will act as coproducer with us on this project.

We have selected Superior Music Inc. to produce the cassettes and CDs. Their competitive prices are important to a project this size and their nearby location offers easy access. Superior is capable of a two-week maximum turnaround on re-orders, at the reduced rate for volume established by our first order.

Promotion and distribution

Promotion of "Lang & Ackroyd: Fiddle & Guitar" will require the production of a television commercial and dubs for each participating television station. Lang & Ackroyd Productions, with considerable experience in broadcast-quality television production, will provide the producer, script, crew, editing, and master, at cost.

We will also require direct-response answering, credit-card payment processing, and shipping and handling services. Since our last promotion, new companies have been formed to handle all these aspects of direct-response promotions. Due, in large part, to the use of electronic banking and credit-card authorization, along with the 800-number telephone services, all these services will be provided by a single supplier, Direct Services Corporation (DSC), which will also receive payments and deposit them in an account for us. For these services, DSC charges an initial fee of $200, plus a monthly fee of $350, plus $7 per unit shipped.

Production Strategy

Remixing

"Lang & Ackroyd: Fiddle & Guitar" will feature 18 all-time favorite fiddle and guitar tunes. The material includes a selection of well-known waltzes, two-steps, bluegrass, and folk instrumentals, such as "Ragtime Annie" and "Apple Blossom Waltz." Since the reproduction rights to most of these songs are in the public domain, a minimum of license fees and royalties will apply.

The material will be remixed to modern standards, and a percussion track will be added, in response to suggestions from previous customers. Direct Services Corp. indicates that cassettes similar to ours outsell CDs at a rate of two to one. Our older customer base is less likely to have switched to the more modern CD format than their younger counterparts. Therefore, we'll order 2,000 cassettes and 1,000 CDs in the first pressing. This gives us the best price break for quantity, while keeping potential losses low should sales be less than expected.

Our new cassette/CD cover design will be bold, brightly colored, and simple, for maximum impact on television. The cover will feature a head-to-waist shot of Jim Lang and Mary Ackroyd, with their instruments, and large upper-case fluorescent pink and blue lettering.

Television commercial

The television commercial will be upbeat, A.M., and hard-sell. Shot on Betacam SP format, it will show the energetic, photogenic Mary

Ackroyd, playing the fiddle tunes advertised.

During our previous promotion, customers informed us that 15 seconds of ordering information was not enough time to write down the necessary information. Therefore, our new commercial will include 20 seconds of ordering information. Furthermore, by using Direct Services Corp., ordering information will be the same for each station, saving us considerable costs in editing and dubbing over our first promotion.

Distribution and Promotion Strategy

Television
We will establish agreements based on per-item (P.I.) arrangements with participating television stations. Under P.I. terms, we will pay 25% of our retail sales, not including shipping and handling, to the stations, which will broadcast the commercials in primarily daytime slots. In our previous venture, we noted that more than 90% of our orders were taken during daytime hours. Our commercial asks customers to allow three weeks for delivery, providing sufficient time for us to re-order, if necessary. Direct Services Corp. will handle all orders and shipping.

Pricing Strategy

There is little room to maneuver prices in direct-response selling. Our prices are in line with similar promotions. We have established a price of $12.99 for cassettes and $16.99 for CDs, plus $3 shipping and handling (S&H). Our shipping and handling charges are 50 cents less per item than those of similar promotions, reflecting our low startup costs.

Financial Strategy

We propose financing the cost of startup and producing the first 3,000 units through a 50-50 arrangement between Lang & Ackroyd Productions and The Bank of New Venture Capital. We would recover all these costs in the first six-month promotion period. The second promotional period — the second year of operation — would be self-sustaining, producing a profit of approximately $15,000.

Fixed costs: Audio production, producing TV commercial, and distribution

Audio production
Producer 500
Studio (8 hours @ $65/hr) 520
Cover design, photography 500
Master cassette 160
Master CD from DAT 275

Audio production costs **$1,955**

Television commercial production
Scripting, producing ($500, waived by L&A)
Camera and sound (one day @ $1,100) **$1,100**
Editing (two hours @ $150) 300
Voiceover (1/2 day minimum)......................................400
Dubs (6 @ $100 each) 600

Television commercial costs......................................**$2,400**

Distribution
Direct Services initial fee **200**
Direct Services, monthly fee, first month **350**

Total fixed costs **$4,905**

Duplication costs
Cassette duplication, cases, covers
   (2,000 copies @ $1.50) 3,000
CD duplication, jackets & box
   (1,000 copies @ $3) 3,000
Licensing fees and royalties 150

Total duplication costs **$6,150**

Total start-up cost $11,055
Financing available from L&A.......................................6,055
Additional financing required **$5,000**
Total possible revenue, first 3,000 units

```
2,000 cassettes @ $12.99.........................................................25,980
1,000 CDs @ $16.99...............................................................16,990
Shipping and handling ($3 x 3,000)..............................................9,000
Total possible revenue, first 3,000 units......................................$51,970
```

Cash Flow Projection

Year One

We anticipate sales of 1,920 cassettes and 960 CDs, for total gross sales (including S&H) in our first year of approximately $50,000:

$$1,920 \times \$15.99 = \$30,700$$
$$960 \times \$19.99 = \underline{\$19,190}$$

Total gross sales: $49,890

The following chart reflects a startup date of December 1. We anticipate a small profit in Year One, as we wish to pay off all startup and financing costs as soon as possible. The second year would see reduced expenses. Since the third year would be the same as the second, it isn't shown. The cash flow chart includes the cost of the first 3,000 units and assumes a re-order will not be necessary until Year Two. After one year, we will have repaid both loans and we will have a small profit.

Cash Flow Chart: Year One

Revenue	Dec	Jan	Feb	Mar	Apr	May	Jun
Startup (loans)	11,055	— — —	— — —	— — —	— — —	— — —	— — —
Cassettes ($13 ea)	— — —	6,240	6,240	6,240	3,120	1,560	1,560
CDs ($17 ea)	— — —	4,080	4,080	4,080	2,040	1,020	1,020
Subtotal	11,055	10,320	10,320	10,320	5,160	2,580	2,580
S&H charges	— — —	2,160	2,160	2,160	1,080	540	540
Total revenue	11,055	12,480	12,480	12,480	6,240	3,120	3,120

Expenses	Dec	Jan	Feb	Mar	Apr	May	Jun
Startup	11,055	— — —	— — —	— — —	— — —	— — —	— — —
DSC monthly fee	— — —	— — —	350	350	350	350	350
DSC per unit fee	— — —	5,040	5,040	5,040	2,520	1,260	1,260
P.I. costs	— — —	2,580	2,580	2,580	1,290	645	645
Bank loan	— — —	900	900	900	900	900	900
L & A loan	— — —	1,000	1,000	1,000	1,000	1,000	1,000
Misc.	— — —	100	100	100	100	100	100
Total expenses	11,055	9,620	9,970	9,970	6,160	4,255	4,255

Cash		Jan	Feb	Mar	Apr	May	Jun
	0	2,860	5,370	7,880	7,960	6,825	5,690

In Year Two, we carry over our profit of $5,690 from Year One, and apply it to our duplication costs. We will have repaid our startup loans, so our costs will be minimal. Year Three (not shown) would be as Year Two. We will have 60 days to pay our duplicating costs, allowing us to cover the $460 deficit by the end of January.

Cash Flow Chart: Year Two

Revenue	Dec	Jan	Feb	Mar	Apr	May	Jun
From Year 1	5,690	– – –	– – –	– – –	– – –	– – –	– – –
Cassettes ($13 ea)	– – –	6,240	6,240	6,240	3,120	1,560	1,560
CDs ($17 ea)	– – –	4,080	4,080	4,080	2,040	1,020	1,020
Subtotal	5,690	10,320	10,320	10,320	5,160	2,580	2,580
S&H charges	– – –	2,160	2,160	2,160	1,080	540	540
Total revenue	5,690	12,480	12,480	12,480	6,240	3,120	3,120

Expenses	Dec	Jan	Feb	Mar	Apr	May	Jun
Duplication costs	6,150	– – –	– – –	– – –	– – –	– – –	– – –
DSC monthly fee	– – –	350	350	350	350	350	350
DSC per unit fee	– – –	5,040	5,040	5,040	2,520	1,260	1,260
P.I. costs	– – –	2,580	2,580	2,580	1,290	645	645
Misc.	– – –	100	100	100	100	100	100
Total expenses	6,150	8,070	8,070	8,070	4,260	2,355	2,355

Cash	(460)	3,950	8,360	12,770	14,750	15,515	16,280

Repayment Schedule

This venture plan supports a request for a $5,000 loan to be amortized over six months, with commensurate monthly payments, beginning in January of Year One. Lang & Ackroyd Productions will guarantee the payments from its parent budget.

Risk Assessment

The enclosed financial statements should ensure Lang & Ackroyd Productions' ability to pay. We are prepared to put up real estate and other chattel to guarantee the loan. Because of our experience in record production and the music industry, we believe our risks in this venture are marginal. The financially healthy Lang & Ackroyd Productions is capable of assuming all financial risks, as described above. We believe we have designed a win-win venture and we invite The Bank of New Venture Capital to participate in it and to profit from it.

LJ MUSIC / page 9

Bedside Reading

If you read for 20 to 30 minutes just before dozing off every night, you'll sleep better and satisfy your need to continue lifelong learning at the same time. Most of the books and magazines below are available at your local bookstore or library.

Books

Cobey, Steven R. *Seven Habits of Highly Effective People*. New York: Simon and Schuster, 1989.

Cullinane, John J. *The Entrepreneur's Survival Guide*. Homewood, Illinois: Irwin, 1993.

Godfrey, Joline. *Our Wildest Dreams*. New York: Harper (Business), 1992.

Halloran, James W. *Why Entrepreneurs Fail*. Blue Ridge Summit, Pennsylvania: Liberty Hall Press (McGraw Hill), 1991.

Nicholas, Ted. *Secrets of Entrepreneurial Leadership*. Dearborn, Michigan: Enterprise, 1993.

Von Oech, Roger. *A Whack on the Side of the Head* (rev.) New York: Warner Books, 1990.

Panabaker, Janet. *Inventing Women: Profiles of Women Inventors*. Toronto: Women Inventors Project, 1991.

Wallace, Liz *The Book for Women Who Invent or Want to*. Toronto: Women Inventors Project, 1989.

Magazines

Business Start-Ups, P.O. Box 58932, Boulder, Colorado 80306

Business Opportunities Handbook, 1020 North Broadway, Suite 111, Milwaukee, Wisconsin 53202

Entrepreneur, Entrepreneur Media Inc., 2392 Morse Ave., Irvine, California 92714

Profit: The Magazine for Canadian Entrepreneurs, CB Media Ltd., 70 The Esplanade, 2nd floor, Toronto, Ontario M5E 1R2

Start Your Own Business, Harris Publications, Inc., 1115 Broadway, New York, N.Y. 10010

Success: The Magazine for Today's Entrepreneurial Mind, 230 Park Ave., New York, N.Y. 10169

Useful Organizations

American Associations

AMBUCS, National Association of American Business Clubs
3315 North Main St., High Point, North Carolina 27265;
(919) 869-2166

American Business Women's Association
9100 Ward Parkway, P.O. Box 8728, Kansas City, Missouri, 64114-0728;
(816) 361-6621

American Federation of Labor and Congress of Industrial Organizations
(AFL-CIO)
815-16th St. N.W., Washington, D.C. 20006; (202) 637-5010

American Institute for Small Business
7515 Wayeata Blvd., St. Louis Park, Minnesota 55426; (612) 545-1984

American Management Association
135 West 50th St., New York, N.Y. 10020-1201; (212) 586-8100

American Society for Testing and Materials
1916 Race St., Philadelphia, Pennsylvania 19103-1187; (215) 299-5400

Center for Entrepreneurial Management
180 Varick St., 17th floor, New York, N.Y. 10014; (212) 633-0060

Committee for Economic Development
477 Madison Ave., New York, N.Y. 10022; (212) 688-2063

Council of Better Business Bureaus
4200 Wilson Blvd., Suite 800, Arlington, Virginia 22203-1804;
(703) 276-0100

Council of Consulting Organizations
521-5th Ave., 35th floor, New York, N.Y. 10175-3598; (212) 697-9693

Creative Education Foundation
1050 Union Rd., #4, Buffalo, N.Y. 14224; (716) 675-3181

Freedom of Information Center
20 Walter Williams Hall, University of Missouri, Columbia, Missouri
65211; (314) 882-4856

International Franchise Association -World Headquarters
1350 New York Ave. N.W., 9th floor, Washington D.C. 20005-4709;
(202) 628-8000

Institute of Management Accountants (formerly the National Association of
Accountants) 10 Paragon Dr., Montvale, New Jersey 07645-1760;
(201) 573-9000

Junior Achievement, Inc.
  1 Education Way, Colorado Springs, Colorado 80906-4477;
  (719) 540-8000

National Association of Manufacturers
  1331 Pennsylvania Ave. N.W., Suite 1500, North Tower, Washington,
  D.C. 20004-1703; (202) 637-3065

National Association of Manufacturers' Agents
  23016 Mill Creek Rd., P.O. Box 3467, Laguna Hills, California 92654;
  (714) 859-4040

National Center for Entrepreneurship in Economic Education
  Calvin A. Kent Center for Private Enterprise, Baylor University, Waco,
  Texas 76798; (817) 755-3766

National Council on Economic Education
  1140 Avenue of the Americas, New York, N.Y. 10036; (212) 730-7007

National Foreign Trade Council
  1270 Avenue of the Americas, New York, N.Y. 10020; (212) 399-7128
  Also: 1625 K St. N.W., Washington, D.C. 20006; (202) 887-0278

The American Society for Quality Control
  611 East Wisconsin Ave., P.O. Box 3005, Milwaukee, Wisconsin
  53201-3005; (414) 272-9575

The United States JayCees (The United States Junior Chamber of
  Commerce)
  P.O. Box 7, Tulsa, Oklahoma 74102-0007; (918) 584-2481

Canadian Associations

Canadian Association of Family Enterprise
7100 Woodbine Ave., Suite 310, Markham, Ontario L3R 5J2;
(905) 940-9646; Fax: 940-8141

Canadian Association of Women Executives and Entrepreneurs
60 Dixon Ave., Toronto, Ontario M4L 1N6; (416) 690-5142

Canadian Bankers' Association
199 Bay St., Commerce Court W., Suite 3000, Toronto, Ontario
M5L 1G2; (416) 362-6092

Canadian Centre for Creative Technology
8 Young St. East, Waterloo, Ontario N2J 2L3; (519) 884-8844

Canadian Chamber of Commerce
55 Metcalfe St., Ottawa, Ontario K1P 6N4; (613) 238-4000

Canadian Council of Better Business Bureaus
1 St. John's Road, Suite 504, Toronto, Ontario M6P 4C7; (416) 922-2584

Canadian Federation of Independent Business
4141 Yonge St., Suite 401, Willowdale, Ontario M2P 2A6;
(416) 222-8022

Canadian Foundation for Economic Education
2 St. Clair Ave. W., Toronto, Ontario M4V 1L5; (416) 968-2236;
Fax: 968-0488

Canadian Franchise Association
5045 Orbiter Dr., Building 12, Unit 201, Mississauga, Ontario L4W 4Y4;
(905) 625-2896; Fax: 625-9076

Canadian Manufacturers Association
75 International Blvd., 4th floor, Toronto, Ontario M9W 6L9;
(416) 798-8000

Canadian Organization of Small Business, Inc.
Box 11246, M.P.O., Edmonton, Alberta T5H 3J5; (403) 423-2672;
Fax: 493-8199

Institute of Certified Management Consultants of Canada
181 Bay St., BCE Place, Heritage Bldg., 2nd floor, P.O. Box 835,
Toronto, Ontario M5J 2T3; (416) 860-1515

Patent and Trademark Institute of Canada
P.O. Box 1298, Station B, Ottawa, Ontario K1P 5R3; (613) 234-0516

Retail Council of Canada
210 Dundas St. W., Suite 600, Toronto, Ontario M5G 2E8;
(416) 598-4684

Women Inventors Project
22 King St. S., Waterloo, Ontario N2J 1N8; (519) 746-3443

List of the Entrepreneurs and Their Ventures

How did you make YOUR breaks?

I'd like to know how you used *Make Your Own Breaks*. I'm also interested in any comments and suggestions you might have about the book. If you'd like to tell me your story, I'd like to hear from you. Send me a letter, or complete the questionnaire below (you may photocopy it, if you wish) and mail to:

Jim Lang
c/o Trifolium Books Inc.
238 Davenport Road, Suite 28
Toronto, Ontario M5R 1J6
Canada

I used your book to make my own breaks by:

_____

_____

_____

I would have liked more information on how to:

_____

_____

_____

I know a great entrepreneur for your next book (aside from me, of course). Here's his/her name, address, and phone number, and a brief description of his/her venture.

_____

_____

_____

I like your book and I know some 11- to 16-year-olds who would love your full-color, illustrated book for young people called *Great Careers for People Who Want to be Entrepreneurs*. I am enclosing $15.95 for a copy (includes GST and shipping). (Send cheque or money order only, please.)

Here's who I am and how to reach me:

Name: _____

Address: _____

Province: _____ Postal Code: _____

Phone: (   ) _____ Fax: (   ) _____